Also by Mark McEwan

Great Food at Home

with Jacob Richler

MARK McEWAN
RUSTIC ITALIAN
Great Italian Recipes Made Easy for Home
WITH JACOB RICHLER

PENGUIN
an imprint of Penguin Canada Books Inc.

Published by the Penguin Group
Penguin Canada Books Inc., 90 Eglinton Avenue East, Suite 700, Toronto, Ontario, Canada M4P 2Y3

Penguin Group (USA) Inc., 375 Hudson Street, New York, New York 10014, U.S.A.
Penguin Books Ltd, 80 Strand, London WC2R 0RL, England
Penguin Ireland, 25 St Stephen's Green, Dublin 2, Ireland (a division of Penguin Books Ltd)
Penguin Group (Australia), 707 Collins Street, Melbourne, Victoria 3008, Australia
(a division of Pearson Australia Group Pty Ltd)
Penguin Books India Pvt Ltd, 11 Community Centre, Panchsheel Park, New Delhi – 110 017, India
Penguin Group (NZ), 67 Apollo Drive, Rosedale, Auckland 0632, New Zealand
(a division of Pearson New Zealand Ltd)
Penguin Books (South Africa) (Pty) Ltd, 24 Sturdee Avenue, Rosebank, Johannesburg 2196, South Africa

Penguin Books Ltd, Registered Offices: 80 Strand, London WC2R 0RL, England

First published in Viking hardcover by Penguin Canada, 2011
Published in this edition, 2013

1 2 3 4 5 6 7 8 9 10

Manufactured in the U.S.A.

Cover and interior design: Mary Opper
Photography: James Tse

LIBRARY AND ARCHIVES CANADA CATALOGUING IN PUBLICATION

McEwan, Mark, 1957–
[Mark McEwan's Fabbrica]
    Rustic Italian : great Italian recipes made easy for home / Mark McEwan with Jacob Richler.

Originally published under title: Mark McEwan's Fabbrica.
    Toronto : Viking Canada, 2011.
Includes index.
ISBN 978-0-14-317749-4 (pbk.)

    1. Cooking, Italian. I. Richler, Jacob, author II. Title.

TX723.M34 2013   641.5945   C2013-905625-4

Visit the Penguin Canada website at **www.penguin.ca**

Special and corporate bulk purchase rates available; please see **www.penguin.ca/corporatesales** or call 1-800-810-3104, ext. 2477.

Contents

Introduction

I opened my newest restaurant, Fabbrica, in the fall of 2010, with a view to serving the most authentic, rustic, regional Italian fare possible. All the recipes included in the pages that follow come from this restaurant. As you will hopefully see, the style of cooking and its ostensible simplicity lends itself particularly well to an accessible cookbook. Many of the recipes can be prepared quickly. But there is plenty here to challenge the home cook, too.

Let me explain. First, as a word of caution, let me say with the authority of someone who has cooked for more than thirty years in the professional kitchen that whether cooking there or at home, the dishes that look the simplest are usually the hardest to get exactly right. There are good reasons for this—especially when it comes to Italian cookery, which generally relies on fewer ingredients to get its message across on the plate than what you find in many other cuisines. Simply put, less on the plate means that what's included had better be very close to perfect. Each element needs to be cooked exactly right. And each ingredient—on display without any rich sauces or distracting clutter to hide behind—must also shine with its freshness and quality.

So when you are cooking these recipes, you may find that they generally challenge you less for the time you need to commit to complete them than for the technique you must possess or practise to make the dish sing. If you are making Grilled Swordfish with Braised Fennel and Orange, no one will be impressed if you left the fish on the grill two minutes too long and it turned out dry, or if you did not properly caramelize the fennel before braising it and so ended up with an absent flavour and a pallid sauce. Nor should you attempt the dish with some pre-sliced, greying, twice-frozen plastic-wrapped piece of swordfish from the pre-packaged section of the supermarket. If instead you take the trouble to find a fresh, quality piece of fish, and get all the other little things right, you need just thirty minutes to turn out a knockout dish.

This book can reward you like that again and again. The best way to ensure that it happens is to never let the book dictate what you go shopping for. Instead, shop first, *then* find a recipe. Always shop with an open mind, and buy only what looks best, freshest, and most seasonally appealing at the market. Then consult the book when you get home. It includes a substantial range of products and ideas. And just as I undertook to do with my cookbook team with our first book, *Great Food at Home*, we have designed the recipes in these pages to be as flexible as possible. Each is welcoming of substitutions in its list of ingredients.

One area where you should never compromise, however, is in the staples—your home larder. Most of the Italian-sourced ingredients we use at Fabbrica are easy to come by everywhere. Using cheaper substitutions is a false economy.

Sure, plum tomatoes from San Marzano, Italy, where they are grown in rich volcanic soil, sun-ripened until tender and sweet, and then harvested exclusively by hand, are always going to cost more than something produced elsewhere in Italy—or for that matter in Canada. As a restaurant owner with an eye on the numbers, I wish that weren't the case. And as a restaurateur whose four restaurants are all in Toronto, Canada, and who seeks to use local products whenever he can, I would be delighted to use a Canadian tomato instead. But as a chef who cares most about how a dish ultimately tastes, I know that a tomato sauce made with San Marzano tomatoes tastes better (sweeter, richer, and less acidic) than one made with any other tomato, and I have no choice but to buy the best.

Likewise, recipes included here for pasta and pizza will turn out better if made with the same Italian "OO" flour we use at the restaurant—not because their wheat or flour is superior to ours, but because as yet no Canadian miller grinds their flour quite as fine. In recipes that call for a particular type of wine—like Pinot Grigio or Barolo—to be used for braising or in a reduction, try to heed the general advice, for in each case the varietal possesses characteristics that lend something special to the finished dish. When it comes to balsamic vinegar, remember that there is no substitute for age and quality.

When a recipe calls for "fine olive oil" with which to season or finish a dish after it has been cooked, use something special—an extra virgin cold-pressed oil of quality (and freshness), for its quality will shine through. But never use such oil in the sauté pan, where it can burn or be otherwise wasted. When a recipe calls for "olive oil," it means oil of the most basic sort. When a recipe calls only for "flour," it means all-purpose flour. "White wine" or "red wine" simply means something dry, of unobjectionable quality. Capers are preferably salt-packed. Unless otherwise specified, "pepper" means freshly ground black pepper. As for "salt," at McEwan restaurants we cook exclusively with the kosher type, because it is pure and mild. You may use any sea salt with similar qualities—but never cook with iodized table salt, which is far too intense for use in cooking.

As for the basic recipes that constitute the building blocks of the featured recipes in the book, I know that most home cooks will cut some corners. All the same, I encourage you to make your own stocks, and especially the flavourful *brodo* that lies at the heart of so many of the soups and braises featured in this book. Take it from me—these recipes will not turn out the same without it. If you simply do not have the time to make it, please never use a bouillon cube or powdered stock in its place—the results will be abysmal. "Homemade" store-prepared stocks are a far better substitute, and you can always reduce them for extra flavour if desired. The other basic recipe well worth making is pasta. Of course this is essential if you are going to make any of the ravioli recipes in this book. But it is also worth the small amount of time and effort required for any of the other pasta dishes. Like stock, it can be easily stored in the freezer. All the same, you are free to use the dry variety as most Italians do!

The last and most important rule of the book is to try to enjoy it in the casual spirit with which it was conceived. These recipes are guidelines, not rigid sets of directions. They should be used as a source of ideas rather than as inflexible instructions as to what you serve at your table. Relax and have a glass of wine while you're cooking. Make it a group affair. There is no surer route to putting a good meal on the table than to have a nice, festive time with friends and family while you make it—and that is true for Italian cooking more than for any other.

Mark McEwan

Zuppe
Soups

Brodo Stock

A *brodo* differs from a typical French stock primarily in that the flavour is driven not by a single meat, but rather by a large variety. The practice doubtlessly originated with a long-simmering stock pot on the corner of a rural Italian stovetop into which all scraps were dispatched for recycling. But the result is perfectly suited to its purpose— as the base for a soup or risotto, or the braising liquid for a meat or vegetable—for the virtue of *brodo* is that it has no distracting star ingredient, only a large supporting cast.

The fantastic recipe for *brodo* that follows is something we owe almost to the letter to the exceptionally talented Marco Canora, the long-time Tom Colicchio protégé who is now executive chef at Hearth, in the East Village, Manhattan. Its only flaw is that while a traditional *brodo* is light-bodied and unassertive, this one is so well rounded in flavour that it can very nearly stand on its own—as in our *stracciatella*. While this surplus of flavour is an asset, it must be deployed judiciously.

Il Brodo di Fabbrica
Fabbrica Chicken Broth

Dark stocks like this one are a product of roasted bones. A simple modification is required when using *brodo* to make risotto, which must be built with a white stock—otherwise the finished dish will be muddy looking. To make a white *brodo* for risotto, simply rinse the chicken bones and do not roast them.

Makes about 5 quarts (5 L)

3 lb (1.5 kg) chicken bones, chopped and rinsed
1 chicken (about 3 lb/1.5 kg), cut into 6 to 8 pieces and rinsed
1 turkey drumstick, rinsed
½ lb (250 g) stewing beef, cut into large cubes and rinsed
1½ cups (375 mL) San Marzano tomatoes
1 leek (white part only), split
2 stalks celery, cut into 2-inch (5 cm) pieces
1 medium carrot, cut into 2-inch (5 cm) pieces
½ bunch parsley
1 tbsp (15 mL) kosher salt
1 tsp (5 mL) black peppercorns

Preheat oven to 450°F (230°C). Pat the chicken bones dry with paper towels, spread them evenly in a shallow roasting pan, and roast, turning periodically, until well browned, about 45 minutes. Transfer the browned bones to a stock pot and add the chicken pieces, turkey, beef, and 8 quarts (8 L) cold water. Bring to a boil, skim the surface well, and lower heat to a simmer. Continue simmering, without stirring, for 20 minutes, frequently skimming impurities from the surface. Add the tomatoes, leek, celery, carrot, parsley, salt, and peppercorns; stir. Simmer, uncovered, for at least 2 more hours, skimming frequently and thoroughly to remove floating rendered fats along with the impurities. Strain the broth through a large chinois or fine-mesh sieve and discard the solids.

Tip: The broth will keep in a sealed container in the refrigerator for 3 days and in the freezer for up to 6 months.

Aigo Bouido
Garlic Soup

From the perspective of cost, this simple dish must be seen to carry the banner for Italian peasant food. Its traditional ingredients—old bread, garlic, and water—are even cheaper and more pedestrian than the handful of basics required for a *spaghetti alla puttanesca*. But they acquire majesty in their symbiosis (especially if you make the profligate choice of using good stock in place of the water). **Serves 6**

2 quarts (2 L) vegetable or chicken stock (page 286)
4 bay leaves
4 juniper berries, crushed
30 cloves garlic, peeled
15 sage leaves
1 tsp (5 mL) thyme leaves
2 cups (500 mL) cubed day-old Italian bread, crusts trimmed
⅓ cup (75 mL) 35% cream
Salt and white pepper

GARNISH
6 slices ciabatta
1 tbsp (15 mL) olive oil
Salt and pepper
Grated Grana Padano or Pecorino Romano
Fine olive oil
Crispy-fried sage leaves (optional; page 278)

Bring the stock to a boil. Wrap the bay leaves and juniper berries in cheesecloth, tie the bundle closed, and add to the stock along with the garlic, sage, and thyme. Return to a boil and then lower heat. Simmer until the garlic is tender, about 30 minutes.

Add the bread and cream. Return to a simmer, stir, and cook for 5 more minutes. Remove spice sachet and blitz the soup in a blender (or with a hand blender). Pass through a strainer if desired. Season to taste.

Sprinkle one side of the ciabatta with some of the olive oil, season, and grill until crisp and golden. Turn, sprinkle with more oil, seasonings, and a little cheese, and grill until crisp and golden. Place the crostini in 6 warm bowls. Pour the soup around the crostini, drizzle with olive oil, sprinkle with sage (optional), and serve.

Zuppa di Pesce
Mediterranean Fish Soup

For obvious reasons, every Mediterranean country boasts at least one distinct take on fish soup. Where the better known bouillabaisse relies on its scorpion-fish and saffron, this Italian take is rooted in variety, and enlivened with basil, chili, and white balsamic vinegar.

Serves 4

1 quart (1 L) fish stock (page 286)
1 tbsp (15 mL) minced onion
1 tbsp (15 mL) minced leek (white part only)
1 tbsp (15 mL) minced fennel
2 tbsp (30 mL) olive oil
1 clove garlic, thinly sliced
16 clams, scrubbed
16 mussels, scrubbed and debearded
¼ cup (60 mL) white wine
¼ tsp (1 mL) chili flakes
1½ cups (375 mL) crushed San Marzano tomatoes
12 basil leaves

4 large scallops, halved crosswise
½ lb (250 g) skinless halibut fillet, quartered
4 medium shrimp, shelled and deveined
4 oz (125 g) cooked octopus (see page 32), sliced
2 tsp (10 mL) white balsamic vinegar
¼ cup (60 mL) chopped parsley
Salt and pepper

GARNISH
4 slices ciabatta, sprinkled with olive oil, seasoned, and toasted
Fine olive oil

In a saucepan, bring the fish stock to a simmer and set aside. In a large sauté pan on medium heat, sweat the onion, leek, and fennel in the olive oil for 3 minutes. Add the garlic and sweat for 3 minutes longer, but do not brown.

Add the clams, mussels, and white wine. Raise the heat to medium-high. Remove the mussels as they pop open and set them aside on a platter. Add the chili flakes, tomatoes, basil leaves, and fish stock. Remove the clams as they pop open and set them aside with the mussels. (Discard any mussels or clams that haven't opened.)

Lower heat to medium-low. Add the scallops and cook gently for 1 minute. Add the halibut and shrimp. A minute or two later, when they are almost fully cooked, remove the scallops, halibut, and shrimp to the platter with the clams and mussels. Add the octopus to the pan just long enough to heat it through. Then stir in the white balsamic vinegar and return all the other seafood to the pot to reheat. Stir in the parsley. Taste and adjust seasonings.

Divide seafood among 4 warm bowls. Pour broth over top. Garnish each bowl with a crostino and follow with a generous drizzle of olive oil.

Substitutions: Any firm white fish, such as monkfish, can stand in for and even upstage the halibut. Shelled lobster or crab will do the same for the shrimp. Or you can increase the variety and include all of them. Choose what you will on the basis of what looks good at the fishmonger, follow the general timing outline for adding and removing molluscs, shellfish, and fish to the pot, and all will turn out well in the end.

Tip: After scrubbing the clams, transfer to a large bowl, fill it with ice water, and stir in 1 tbsp (15 mL) of cornmeal. In order to encourage them to give up their grit, leave the clams to snack on that for 20 minutes. Then drain and rinse.

Stracciatella alla Romana
Chicken Broth and Egg Drop Soup

This simple soup from the Roman oeuvre is a classic that too often does not taste that way—invariably because the chef took a shortcut with the stock. But if you make it properly, beginning with our *brodo*, you will grasp the elusive genius of the dish at the first spoonful. **Serves 6**

2 quarts (2 L) *brodo* (page 3)
3 eggs
3 tbsp (50 mL) grated Parmigiano-Reggiano
1 tbsp (15 mL) minced parsley
Pinch of nutmeg
Salt and pepper

GARNISH
Minced parsley
Freshly grated Parmigiano-Reggiano

Bring the broth to a boil in a saucepan over high heat and then lower to a simmer. Meanwhile, in a bowl combine the eggs, Parmesan, and parsley and beat together with a fork. Swiftly transfer the mixture to the simmering soup and allow it to cook undisturbed until it rises to the surface and forms a raft, about 2 minutes. Break up the raft with a fork, then season the soup to taste. Serve the soup with bowls of parsley and Parmesan on the side.

Tip: If you prefer ribbons of egg in the broth, stir the soup with a fork as you add the egg mixture rather than leaving it undisturbed to form a raft.

Zuppa di Cavolo Nero, Salsiccia e Fagioli
Kale, Sausage, and Bean Soup

Kale is credited with lowering cholesterol, which means, as we understand it, that you can eat it with sausage and end up square. More importantly, this robust soup, with its healthful mix of beans, kale, and nourishing broth, is a complete meal in a bowl, with a surplus of flavour to boot. **Serves 6**

3 tbsp (50 mL) olive oil
1 medium Spanish onion, diced
2 stalks celery, diced
1 large carrot, diced
8 cloves garlic, minced
Leaves from 5 sprigs thyme, minced
2 bay leaves
1 tbsp (15 mL) fennel seeds, toasted
1 tsp (5 mL) chili flakes
4 mild Italian sausages (about 2 lb/1 kg), casings removed
2 bunches black kale, stems and centre ribs removed, leaves roughly chopped
1 can (28 oz/796 mL) San Marzano tomatoes, crushed
3 quarts (3 L) *brodo* (page 3)
Salt and pepper
1 can (19 oz/540 mL) cannellini beans, rinsed and drained
2 tbsp (30 mL) sherry vinegar

Heat the oil in a soup pot on medium-high heat. Add the onion, celery, and carrot and cook, stirring frequently, until wilted but not coloured. Add the garlic, thyme, bay leaves, fennel seeds, and chili flakes; sauté for 1 minute longer. Add the sausage. Break up the meat with a wooden spoon and stir vigorously until it is lightly browned. Add the kale and tomatoes, and continue to cook until the tomato juices have reduced by about three-quarters. Add the *brodo*, season lightly, and simmer, partially covered, for 1½ hours.

Add the beans, stir in the vinegar, and adjust the seasonings. Add more chili flakes if desired. Serve with a good crusty loaf of rustic bread.

Fagioli Beans

When it arrived from the New World in the early sixteenth century, the fantastically healthful legume we know as the bean was collectively embraced by all the different peoples of what would later become Italy. But none showed quite such unrelenting enthusiasm as the Tuscans—to this day, other Italians disparagingly refer to them as *mangiafagioli* ("bean eaters"). There, it is the cannellini—or white kidney bean—that enjoys the greatest popularity, and it is thus the only choice for a proper Tuscan bean soup. In the northern Veneto region, another hotbed of bean-enthusiasm, the most treasured variety is the crimson-speckled lamon. This geographically specific borlotti (or cranberry) bean is the essential ingredient for an equally celebrated Venetian soup, *pasta e fagioli*. In Umbria, local preference instead runs to lentils. In Abruzzi and Lazio, they prefer *ceci* (chickpeas) and fava beans.

None of these varieties are as widely or reliably available fresh in North America as they are in Italy, which too often leaves the Canadian cook to choose between beans that are dried or canned. Each has different drawbacks. Dried beans are generally superior to canned ones in flavour and texture—but not when they are old and stale, so buy dried beans exclusively from a supplier with high turnover. Canned varieties of high quality are far more consistent. But never economize—cheap canned beans are often soft and pulpy.

Minestra di Cannellini
Tuscan White Bean Soup

Tuscan bean soup is not typically puréed and you need not do so if you prefer the rustic approach. But this refined smooth version, with pesto providing a lift in colour and flavour, is a most satisfying interpretation. **Serves 6**

1 cup (250 mL) top-quality dried cannellini beans
2 tbsp (30 mL) olive oil
2 leeks (white part only), chopped
1 stalk celery, chopped
1 medium carrot, chopped
½ medium onion, sliced
6 sage leaves, cut in half
3 bay leaves
1 tsp (5 mL) minced rosemary
3 quarts (3 L) chicken stock (page 286)
Salt and pepper

GARNISH
¼ cup (60 mL) basil pesto (page 281)
Fine olive oil

Pick over the beans, transfer to a bowl, and cover generously with cold water. Soak overnight, changing the water 2 or 3 times. Drain and rinse the beans.

Heat the oil in a soup pot on medium-low heat. Add the leeks, celery, carrot, and onion, and sweat until completely wilted, stirring frequently to prevent them from browning. Stir in the sage, bay leaves, and rosemary. Cook gently for 2 minutes, then add the beans and stock. Raise the heat, bring to a boil, and then lower heat to a simmer. Season with pepper—but not salt, which will toughen the beans. Cook, uncovered, until the beans are tender but not yet losing their skins and growing mushy, about 1 hour.

Discard the bay leaves. Purée the soup in a blender (or with a hand blender) until smooth, and then pass it through a sieve into a clean pot. Taste and adjust seasonings. Serve each bowl dabbed with about 1 tsp (5 mL) pesto and a drizzle of olive oil. Accompany with crusty bread.

Substitutions: Other quality white beans may be used in place of the cannellini. Vegetable stock may be used in place of the chicken stock. *Brodo* will work too, though its extra flavour is not required and would thus arguably be squandered.

Insalate
Salads

Tonno Tuna

The Mediterranean features diminishing numbers of the same bluefin and albacore tuna that lurk off the east and west coasts of Canada. These awesomely muscular fish can swim up to 100 kilometres per hour and, as a product of their associated voracious appetite, can reach a weight of 5 kilograms in their first year (a lobster, by contrast, takes seven years to reach a weight of 500 grams). A couple of thousand years before Canadians took to sport fishing for the great bluefin, and then posing with their prey for a quick snapshot before tossing it into the nearest ditch to rot, the Romans were commemorating their respect and awe for their tuna by decorating vases with its image, which they also stamped on coins and built into their mosaics.

The practice described here of poaching fresh tuna in stock and then preserving it in jars filled with olive oil used to be common up and down the coastal communities of Italy. Then, like most home preserves, it was supplanted by industrially produced versions. Naturally homemade is much tastier than any you can buy. But if you insist on giving it a pass, do what so many Italians do and buy only tuna of quality packed in olive oil—and never the cheap, hopelessly bland variety that is preserved in vegetable stock or water.

Tonno Sott'Olio
Olive-Oil-Preserved Tuna

1 small fennel bulb, julienned
1 medium red onion, julienned
2 stalks celery, sliced
1 medium carrot, sliced
4 bay leaves (preferably fresh)
1 tbsp (15 mL) fennel seeds
1 tsp (5 mL) kosher salt
1 tsp (5 mL) black peppercorns
1 fillet (1 lb/500 g) albacore (or yellowfin) tuna
2 Anaheim (or 4 Thai) chilies, sliced
3 cups (750 mL) olive oil

In a large saucepan, combine the fennel, onion, celery, carrot, bay leaves, fennel seeds, salt, peppercorns, and 3 quarts (3 L) cold water. Bring to a boil, lower heat, and simmer for 15 minutes. Add the tuna and simmer until just cooked through, about 7 minutes. Remove the tuna from the poaching liquid to a plate, cover with plastic wrap, and let cool on the countertop for 30 minutes. Transfer tuna to a 1-quart (1 L) Mason jar or other sealable container. Add the chilies and enough of the olive oil to completely submerge the fish. Seal the jar and leave to steep at room temperature for 2 hours. Transfer to the refrigerator, where the tuna will keep for a month.

Tip: At McEwan Fine Foods, when we prepare preserved tuna for sale in Mason jars, for a nice presentation we pack the tuna with sliced lime, sliced lemon, fennel fronds, and bay leaves. If you choose to do the same, the tuna will have a diminished shelf life of only 2 weeks.

Suggested Wine: Sicilian white

Insalata di Scarola con Tonno, Arancia e Ravanello
Escarole Salad with Preserved Tuna, Orange, and Radish

Meaty tuna combines so well with the mild bitterness of escarole and the bright, refreshing notes of orange and crunchy radish that this salad adds up to a perfect lunch for a sunny summer day. **Serves 4**

1 large head escarole, torn
8 leaves radicchio (Verona or Treviso), torn
¼ cup (60 mL) mixed celery and parsley leaves
Leaves from 2 sprigs oregano, chopped
4 peppery radishes, sliced on a mandoline
2 cups (500 mL) flaked preserved tuna (page 19)
3 seedless oranges, peeled
½ cup (125 mL) Roasted Garlic Dressing (page 27)
Chopped chives or micro greens

In a wooden salad bowl, combine the escarole, radicchio, parsley, oregano, radishes, and tuna. Using a very sharp knife, and working over the salad bowl so that the juices fall into it, cut the orange segments out from between their membranes and let them drop onto the salad. Toss. Dress salad with about half the dressing, and toss again. Garnish with a scattering of chives. Wipe clean the edges of the bowl and serve the salad with the extra dressing on the side.

Substitution: You can make this salad with canned tuna—but use only the finest Italian olive-oil-packed kind.

Suggested Wine: Sicilian white

Insalata di Tonno e Fagioli
Preserved Tuna with Tuscan Bean Salad

Tuna and beans are a classic Italian flavour combination. Here we enhance the mix by combining our own flavourful preserved tuna with a full-fledged Tuscan bean salad. It makes a splendid and healthful first course for a summertime lunch. Serves 6

2 cans (each 28 oz/796 mL) cannellini, romano, lupini, white kidney, or other quality white beans
3 cups (750 mL) flaked preserved tuna (page 19)
2 large ripe Roma tomatoes, cored and diced
½ English cucumber, seeded and diced
1 stalk celery, thinly sliced diagonally
Leaves from ¼ bunch parsley, chopped
Leaves from ¼ bunch basil, chopped
Juice of 1 lemon
1 cup (250 mL) fine olive oil
½ cup (125 mL) white balsamic vinegar
Salt and pepper

Rinse the beans, drain them thoroughly, and transfer to a large bowl. Set aside 1 cup (250 mL) of the tuna and add the balance to the beans. Follow with the tomatoes, cucumber, celery, parsley, basil, lemon juice, olive oil, and balsamic vinegar. Season, and toss well. Set aside for 30 minutes for the flavours to blend. Toss again, taste, and adjust seasonings. Serve topped with the reserved tuna.

Variation: Omit the tuna and serve a classic—and vegetarian—Tuscan bean salad.

Substitutions: You can use dried beans for this dish and soak, cook, and cool them. In place of the preserved tuna, you may use canned, but if you expect a dish of quality, you must use the finest available tuna of Italian origin, and packed in olive oil—not vegetable oil or stock or water.

Suggested Wine: Vernaccia di San Gimignano

Insalata Misticanza
Mixed Lettuce Salad

This salad offers a bracingly refreshing combination of flavours and textures. But do not feel obliged to follow the recipe to the letter and go out of your way to seek out every lettuce on the list. What's important is to stay faithful to the basic idea, and to present a similarly varied and pleasing combination of contrasting flavours and textures.

Serves 6 to 8

1 small head radicchio, torn
1 small head lollo rosso lettuce, torn
1 small head red oak leaf lettuce, torn
1 package baby romaine leaves (or 1 head, youngest leaves only), torn
1 large handful escarole leaves, torn
1 large handful baby arugula, stems trimmed
1 large handful frisée, torn
1 cup (250 mL) shaved fennel
1 celery stalk, shaved on a mandoline
Leaves from ¼ bunch basil, torn
Leaves from ¼ bunch parsley, torn
1 cup (250 mL) House Dressing (page 27)

Combine the lettuces, fennel, celery, basil, and parsley and toss. Add half the dressing and toss again. Serve with the remaining dressing on the side.

Aceto Balsamico Balsamic Vinegar

Whether applied to freshly butchered beef on the hook, to young cheese, or to wine in the cellar, time is the single essential ingredient that has no substitute in its effect—on flavour, and on price. So it is with balsamic vinegar, only more so.

The finest balsamic vinegars from Modena have been barrel-aged for many decades—and occasionally for a century or more. These vinegars begin life as grape must. The pale juice from the first pressing and first stage of winemaking is reduced by a third to a half and then introduced to the aging barrel. The barrels are placed in the attic, so as to be better exposed to the rigours of the local climate, from hot summers that encourage evaporation to chilly, mellowing winters. Just like raw whiskey or rum, the vinegar acquires most of its colour and flavour from the wood of its barrel. And of these, the vinegar encounters a succession, for as

evaporation causes its volume to shrink and its flavour to intensify, the liquid is transferred to smaller and smaller vessels, each fashioned from a different type of wood, and possessing a different character. The end product is richly aromatic and thick like syrup, its flavour a perfect balance of sweetness and acidity.

Fine balsamic vinegar is intended to be used sparingly, from a few drops to a small drizzle over anything from a salad to a bowl of strawberries or even ice cream. It is intended not to be used in cooking or preparing a dish, but in finishing it, so that—as with a white truffle—its aroma and flavour may grace the dish uncorrupted.

Roasted Garlic Dressing

Makes about 2 cups (500 mL)

3 heads garlic
1 tbsp (15 mL) basic olive oil
Salt and pepper
1 cup (250 mL) fine olive oil
½ cup (125 mL) white wine vinegar
½ cup (125 mL) rice wine vinegar

1 tbsp (15 mL) liquid honey
Leaves from ¼ bunch oregano, minced
1 tbsp (15 mL) dried basil
¾ tsp (4 mL) kosher salt
½ tsp (2 mL) pepper

Preheat oven to 325°F (160°C). Slice off and discard the bottom ¼ inch (5 mm) of each head of garlic. Smear a sheet of foil with half of the basic olive oil, arrange the garlic bottom down, and drizzle with the rest of the basic oil. Season lightly. Fold over the foil, seal it tightly, and place on a baking sheet. Roast until the garlic is tender, about 45 minutes.

Cool for 10 minutes, then squeeze the garlic into a large bowl. Add the fine olive oil, vinegars, honey, oregano, basil, and salt and pepper; whisk thoroughly. Set aside to steep for at least an hour. Strain the vinaigrette into a clean container. Before using, whisk again and adjust seasonings.

House Dressing

Makes about 1¹/₂ cups (375 mL)

1 cup (250 mL) fine olive oil
⅓ cup (75 mL) red wine vinegar
2 tbsp (30 mL) white balsamic vinegar
Salt and pepper

In a large bowl, thoroughly whisk together the oil and vinegars. Season to taste. Just before using, whisk again.

Gorgonzola Dressing

Makes about 2¹/₂ cups (625 mL)

½ cup (125 mL) sour cream
4 oz (125 g) gorgonzola
4 oz (125 g) Danish blue
Juice of 1 lemon
1 tbsp (15 mL) caramelized onion
¾ cup (175 mL) buttermilk

¼ cup (60 mL) olive oil
1 tsp (5 mL) liquid honey
½ tsp (2 mL) Worcestershire sauce
¼ tsp (1 mL) hot pepper sauce
Salt and pepper

In a blender, combine the sour cream, gorgonzola, blue cheese, lemon juice, and onion; blend until smooth. Transfer to a bowl and whisk in the buttermilk, olive oil, honey, Worcestershire sauce, hot sauce, and salt and pepper. Taste and adjust seasonings.

Insalata di Cicoria con Olive e Caciocavallo
Dandelion Salad with Olives and Caciocavallo

The Italian salad repertoire features many that possess an assertively bitter flavour profile, and this is one of our favourite examples. Despite its scant list of ingredients, it packs a wallop of flavour. The sharp and salty nature of a well-aged artisanal caciocavallo from Sicily is a league apart from that of even the finest caciocavallo from Calabria or anywhere else on the mainland, so do make the effort to find one. **Serves 4**

2 bunches dandelion leaves, torn
1 handful parsley leaves
1 cup (250 mL) small quality olives, pitted
¼ cup (60 mL) aged wine vinegar
2 tbsp (30 mL) fine olive oil
Salt and pepper
4 oz (125 g) Caciocavallo Siciliano

In a salad bowl, combine the dandelion, radicchio, parsley, and olives. Toss. Add vinegar, oil, and salt and pepper, and toss again. Taste and correct seasonings. Shave half the caciocavallo over the salad, and serve with the extra cheese on the side.

Insalata con Bistecca
Skirt Steak Salad

This salad, with a small, flavoursome steak, makes for a perfect cottage lunch-in-one. If you want to feed more than the two people suggested, simply multiply the recipe. But keep in mind that skirt steak—as with any substitute cut, like flank, hanger, or flat-iron—toughens unpalatably when cooked beyond rare. So if you are simultaneously cooking six of them, be wary and be quick: by the time the sixth one lands on the grill, the first will be ready for flipping. **Serves 2**

2 top-quality skirt steaks (each about 5 oz/150 g)
¼ cup (60 mL) Roasted Garlic Dressing (page 27)
Salt and pepper
4 cups (1 L) lightly packed peppery young arugula
¼ cup (60 mL) shaved fennel
4 leaves radicchio (Verona or Treviso), torn
1 small handful celery leaves
1 small handful combined parsley, torn basil, and oregano leaves
4 slices bresaola, torn
2 tbsp (30 mL) olive oil
2 tsp (10 mL) balsamic vinegar
¼ cup (60 mL) julienned pickled onion
8 halves smoked (or oil-packed sun-dried) tomato
Cracked black pepper

GARNISH
8 basil leaves
Parmigiano-Reggiano or Pecorino Romano shavings
1 tbsp (15 mL) balsamic reduction (optional; page 274)

Place the steaks and dressing in a sealable container, turn meat a few times to coat, and marinate in the refrigerator for 24 hours. Let sit at room temperature for 30 minutes before grilling.

Preheat grill on high.

Remove the steaks from the marinade, shaking off any excess, and season them generously on both sides. Grill the steaks until rare. Transfer to a cutting board, cover loosely with foil, and let rest for about 5 minutes.

Meanwhile, in a bowl combine the arugula, fennel, radicchio, celery leaves, mixed herbs, and bresaola. Whisk together oil and balsamic vinegar, season, pour over salad, and toss well. Divide the salad between 2 plates. Top each with the pickled onion, tomato, and cracked black pepper.

Slice each steak against the grain into strips about ¼ inch (5 mm) thick. Place each sliced steak alongside the salad and drizzle steaks with the juices from the cutting board. Garnish each salad with basil leaves, cheese shavings, and, if you choose, drizzle the whole plate with the balsamic reduction.

Suggested Wine: Barbera d'Asti

Polpi e Ceci
Charred Octopus with Chickpeas

From beating the regrettable creature against the rocks to boiling it with corks, popular methods for tenderizing the octopus are varied and numerous. They are also largely redundant, as octopus generally arrives at market pre-tenderized (usually, they do time in a cement mixer with rocks for company). Regardless, the unusual method of cooking octopus described here yields a flawlessly tender result every time. **Serves 4**

¾ cup (175 mL) olive oil
½ bunch parsley
3 cloves garlic, sliced
1 small octopus (about 3 lb/1.5 kg)
1½ cups (375 mL) canned chickpeas, rinsed and well drained
¼ cup (60 mL) julienned salami
2 tbsp (30 mL) peperonata (page 279)
1 tbsp (15 mL) chopped parsley
1 tbsp (15 mL) chopped oregano
1 tbsp (15 mL) fine olive oil
1 tsp (5 mL) lemon juice
Salt and pepper
2 tbsp (30 mL) red wine vinegar
½ tbsp (7 mL) minced oil-preserved red chilies
1½ cups (375 mL) peppery young arugula, roughly chopped
1 green onion, thinly sliced

In a large saucepan over low heat, combine ½ cup (125 mL) of the olive oil and the parsley and garlic. Add the octopus, cover, and simmer for 1½ hours or until the octopus is tender and a knife easily penetrates its flesh where the arms join the head. Allow the octopus to cool in the oil, then cut off its arms and discard the head. Set aside 4 tentacles, saving the rest for another purpose. Refrigerate until needed.

Preheat grill on high.

Meanwhile, in a large bowl, combine the chickpeas, salami, peperonata, parsley, oregano, fine olive oil, lemon juice, and salt and pepper; toss well. Taste and adjust seasonings. In a small bowl, whisk together the remaining ¼ cup (60 mL) of olive oil with the red wine vinegar and chilies. Season with salt and pepper, taste, and correct seasonings.

Oil the grill and lightly char 4 octopus tentacles on both sides. Cut the tentacles on the diagonal into slices about 1 inch (2.5 cm) thick. Toss the octopus in the chili vinaigrette. Add the arugula to the chickpea salad and toss again. Transfer to a platter and arrange the octopus slices on top. Garnish with a scattering of green onions and serve.

Suggested Wine: Gavi

Insalata di Pollo Arrosto, Mele e Gorgonzola
Roast Chicken Salad with Apples and Gorgonzola Dressing

Needless to say, this Italianized Waldorf salad would make a great home for any leftover roast chicken. But the sweet, flavour-infused flesh of the brined bird in this recipe very much elevates the resulting mix. So if you are feeding a casual summer lunch to a handful of friends, do try making this salad from the beginning rather than merely using it as a pleasant destiny for leftovers. **Serves 6**

½ cup (125 mL) kosher salt

½ cup (125 mL) brown sugar

1 tbsp (15 mL) yellow mustard seeds

2 bay leaves

1 small top-quality chicken (about 3 lb/1.5 kg)

1 tbsp (15 mL) combined minced sage, thyme, rosemary, and parsley

1 clove garlic, minced

2 tbsp (30 mL) olive oil

Salt and pepper

6 cups (1.5 L) lightly packed peppery young arugula

Leaves from 6 Belgian endives, sliced on diagonal about ½ inch (1 cm) thick

12 leaves radicchio, torn

½ head escarole, torn

Leaves from ¼ bunch parsley

Leaves from ¼ bunch oregano, chopped

1 stalk celery, shaved on a mandoline

1 large (or 1½ medium) Granny Smith apple, julienned

½ cup (125 mL) chopped toasted walnuts

2 cups (500 mL) Gorgonzola Dressing (page 27)

GARNISH

½ cup (125 mL) crumbled gorgonzola, at room temperature

1 green onion, thinly sliced on the diagonal

In a large saucepan, combine the salt, sugar, mustard seeds, bay leaves, and 2 quarts (2 L) cold water. Bring to a boil, stirring until the sugar and salt have dissolved. Chill. Submerge the chicken in the cold brine and refrigerate for 24 hours.

Preheat oven to 375°F (190°C).

Remove the chicken from the brine, discarding the brine. Rinse the chicken under cold running water and pat dry; place in a small roasting pan. Stir together the minced herbs, garlic, and olive oil and rub the paste all over the chicken, inside and out. Season the bird, and roast, untrussed, until done, about 1 hour. Let cool to room temperature. Remove and discard skin. Shred the meat from the carcass in bite-sized morsels; set aside.

In a wooden salad bowl, combine the arugula, endives, radicchio, escarole, parsley, oregano, celery, apple, and walnuts. Reserve 1 cup (250 mL) of the shredded chicken and add the balance to the salad. Toss well. Dress with about half the gorgonzola dressing—or to taste—and toss again. Wipe clean the edges of the bowl. Top the salad with the reserved chicken, crumbled gorgonzola, and green onions. Serve with extra dressing on the side.

Suggested Wine: Italian Chardonnay

Antipasti
Starters

Crostini
Small Toasted Bread

The four crostini toppings that follow demonstrate something of the enormous range of good, strong flavours that can fit on a small piece of fine toast. Each recipe is designed to make a dozen crostini. Two or three types—one of them vegetarian—share space beautifully on a platter passed around with cocktails. **Makes 12 crostini**

½ slender ciabatta, sliced ½ inch (1 cm) thick
2 tbsp (30 mL) olive oil
Sea salt and pepper

Preheat broiler. Arrange the ciabatta slices on a baking sheet, sprinkle with half the olive oil, and season with salt and pepper. Broil until crisp and golden. Turn and repeat. (You can make these ahead and store for a day or so in an airtight container—but not in humid weather.)

Flaked Tuna with White Beans and Olive Salsa

1 cup (250 mL) canned or jarred cannellini beans,
    rinsed and drained
2 tbsp (30 mL) fine olive oil
1 tbsp (15 mL) aged wine vinegar
¼ tsp (1 mL) sugar
Salt and pepper
½ cup (125 mL) brined green olives, rinsed,
    drained, pitted, and chopped
6 halves oil-packed sun-dried tomatoes, chopped
4 anchovy fillets, chopped

1 tbsp (15 mL) capers, rinsed, drained, and chopped
1 small clove garlic, minced
Leaves from ¼ bunch parsley, chopped
12 leaves basil, torn
2 tbsp (30 mL) olive oil
1 tbsp (15 mL) red wine vinegar
½ tbsp (7 mL) lemon juice
1 cup (250 mL) flaked preserved tuna (page 19),
    oil reserved
1 cup (250 mL) baby arugula (or parsley)

In a blender, combine the beans, fine olive oil, aged wine vinegar, and sugar. Season and then purée. Taste, correct seasonings, and set aside.

In a bowl, combine the olives, tomatoes, anchovies, capers, garlic, parsley, and basil; mix well with a spoon. Add olive oil, red wine vinegar, and lemon juice; mix again. Season—but salt lightly in deference to the anchovies and capers. Mix, correct seasonings, and set aside.

Spread the white bean purée on the crostini. Mound with the tuna flakes, and top with a generous sprinkle of the olive salsa. To finish, sprinkle with a little of the reserved tuna oil, and top with the arugula.

Tomato and Buffalo Mozzarella

6 Roma tomatoes, prepared as for passato (page 83), coarsely chopped
2 small balls fresh mozzarella di bufala, cubed
1 cup basil leaves, loosely packed, torn
Fine olive oil

Preheat oven to 350°F (180°C). Arrange crostini on a baking sheet. Spoon the tomato over the toast; follow with the cheese, and then transfer to the oven until cheese melts—about 3 minutes. Garnish with basil and a sprinkle of olive oil.

Gorgonzola Torta and Mushrooms

¾ cup (175 mL) mascarpone, at room temperature
2 oz (60 g) gorgonzola, at room temperature
1 tbsp (15 mL) olive oil
2 cups (500 mL) beech or other top-quality mushroom, trimmed
Generous pinch of minced rosemary
Squeeze of lemon juice
Salt and pepper

Make the torta by folding the gorgonzola into the mascarpone until smooth; set aside. Sauté the mushrooms in the olive oil until wilted. Add the rosemary, deglaze with lemon juice, and season. Spread the gorgonzola torta on the crostini. Slice or quarter any mushrooms that seem excessively large, then heap them over the torta.

Marrow Butter and Horseradish Gremolata

1 batch bone marrow butter (page 275)
1 batch horseradish gremolata (page 278)

Spread a layer of marrow butter on the crostini. Sprinkle generously with horseradish gremolata.

Salumi Cured Meats

The word *salumi* shares its etymological root with *sale*, which means salt and is the one thing that all salumi have in common. Whether cooked (like mortadella), air-dried (prosciutto di Parma), or smoked (soppressata—usually), all salumi are first cured with salt. The other virtual constant—with the exception of bresaola—is that salumi are made with pork. From brawn (soppressata) to the neck (coppa) to the feet (zampone) to the leg (prosciutto), every piece of the animal can be and is used for some sort of salumi. So it is that in Italy, pigs are bred and fed with a view to how they will taste when cured, not fresh, for it is the former that is of far greater importance. The Italian propensity for curing pork is so renowned that even in France, many *charcutières* are

of Italian heritage. Fortunately, Italian Canadians often possess the same gift. So our long dependency on imported Italian salumi has been broken of late by local artisans, like Mario Pingue, of Niagara Foods Specialties, and the incomparable Alfredo Santangelo, who prepares so many of our excellent salumi for Fabbrica.

Ricotta Fresca con Fichi e Miele
Fresh Ricotta with Figs and Honey

Unlike other cheeses, which require rennet, lipose powder, and other elusive ingredients for their preparation, fresh ricotta requires only the basic ingredients. The process is easy, and the result light, creamy, and delicious. Try it. **Serves 6**

1 quart (1 L) 2% milk
1 cup (250 mL) 35% cream
½ tsp (2 mL) salt
3 tbsp (50 mL) lemon juice
1 ciabatta, sliced ½ inch (1 cm) thick
¼ cup (60 mL) olive oil
Salt and pepper
12 ripe figs, quartered
2 tbsp (30 mL) chestnut flower honey (or other quality liquid)
Fine olive oil
Flaky sea salt

In a large saucepan, combine the milk, cream, and salt; bring to a rolling boil. Stir in the lemon juice and lower heat to a simmer; simmer for 2 to 3 minutes. Pour into a cheesecloth-lined strainer over the sink. Place the strainer over a bowl and leave to drain for 1 hour. Serve tepid, right away, or store, covered, in the refrigerator.

Sprinkle both sides of the ciabatta slices with the olive oil, salt, and pepper; toast until crisp and golden. Mound the fresh ricotta at the centre of a large platter. Surround it with the figs, encircled with the crostini. Drizzle the ricotta with the honey and fine olive oil, sprinkle with salt, and serve.

Suggested Wine: Moscato d'Asti

Giardiniera
Pickled Mixed Vegetables

With modern supermarkets perennially overflowing with bounty, the practice of pickling is now more one of taste than necessity. No matter. The taste can be superb—as in this recipe, where vegetables are blanched in no fewer than three different vinegars, and then vibrantly seasoned. **Makes 1 large platter**

1 cup (250 mL) cider vinegar
1 cup (250 mL) champagne vinegar
1 cup (250 mL) aged wine vinegar
1 cup (250 mL) sugar
2 tbsp (30 mL) salt
1 tbsp (15 mL) dried oregano
1 tbsp (15 mL) dried basil
1 tsp (5 mL) chili flakes
2 bay leaves
1 fennel bulb, trimmed, cut lengthwise into ½-inch (1 cm) slices
1 large carrot, peeled, halved lengthwise, cut into ¼-inch (5 mm) slices
½ head cauliflower, cut into florets
1 red bell pepper, cored, cut into ½-inch (1 cm) strips
1 yellow bell pepper, cored, cut into ½-inch (1 cm) strips
1½ cups (375 mL) olive oil
¼ cup (60 mL) chopped parsley
Pinch each of dried oregano and chili flakes

In a saucepan, combine the cider vinegar, champagne vinegar, wine vinegar, sugar, salt, oregano, basil, chili flakes, and bay leaves. Bring to a boil over high heat, stirring until sugar and salt have dissolved. Working with one vegetable at a time, blanch the fennel, carrot, cauliflower, and bell peppers in the vinegar mixture until they are barely tender—no more than 1 minute—and then transfer them to a large baking sheet to cool in a single layer.

Strain the vinegar mixture. Transfer ½ cup (125 mL) to the refrigerator to chill; discard the rest. In a large bowl, whisk together the olive oil and chilled vinegar mixture. Add the vegetables, and toss by hand to coat thoroughly. Transfer the vegetables to a platter and sprinkle with the parsley, oregano, and chili flakes. (If you do not wish to use them immediately, transfer to a sealable nonreactive container and store in the refrigerator for up to 1 month.)

Substitutions: Needless to say, other colours of bell peppers may be substituted for the red and yellow. Any kind of cauliflower will work. Other firm vegetables, like celery and parsnip, can be substituted for the fennel and carrot. Use your imagination—just remember to keep the mix colourful.

Suggested Wine: beer

Olives

The contemporary reach of olive cultivation extends from Australia to California and South Africa, but the fruit will always remain fundamentally identified with the region of its origin, the Mediterranean, for which it is both a staple and a symbol. As the ancient Greeks told it, Athena delivered them the original olive tree, which sprouted on the Acropolis, but it seems more likely that the tree was first cultivated in Syria, from where it spread with the usual unstoppable alliance of inquisitive farmers and hungry birds spreading seed. In any event, the olive tree was entrenched in Italy in time to constitute the longest, most important section of that seminal work on organic agriculture, *On Farming*, which Cato scratched down circa 175 BC. Almost ever since, Italy has been a leading producer and is rivalled today only by Spain.

Olives grown for oil are always harvested in late autumn, when they are soft, very ripe, and black. Olives picked for the table may also be picked then—or, for different effect, much earlier, when young, firm, and green, or in between, and just ripe, when the softening fruit has turned purple. Once harvested, they may be cured in water, brine, salt, oil, or lye. The myriad types of table olives are a combined product of strain, ripeness, and cure. Alas, there is no strict system for their classification. Usually, they are named for their place of origin, as with Gaeta or Cerignola—but then, some places specialize in more than one type. Olives may also be labelled for their variety, like Salona, or even their cure, like Sicilian-style, which usually indicates a marinade rich with herbs. The only reliable route to overcoming the confusion on the label is a splendid journey of taste and experimentation.

Olive di Cerignola Marinate
Marinated Cerignola Olives

The practice of enhancing the flavour of olives by adding aromatic herbs and other seasonings to their brine goes back many centuries. Here we instead finish brined olives in flavoured olive oil for an excellent result. When the olives are all gone, keep the oil: it can be used again and also makes a superb fragrant seasoning oil.

1 quart (1 L) olive oil
6 sprigs parsley
4 sprigs rosemary
6 cloves garlic, thinly sliced
Zest of 2 lemons
3 Anaheim (or 6 Thai) chilies, thinly sliced
1 tbsp (15 mL) chili flakes
1 tbsp (15 mL) fennel seeds
1 lb (500 g) brined green Cerignola olives

In a saucepan gently heat the oil to a temperature of 275°F (140°C). Remove from heat and add the parsley, rosemary, garlic, zest, chilies, chili flakes, and fennel seeds. Use a wooden spoon to completely submerge all the flavourings, and then steep, uncovered, for 1 hour.

Meanwhile, rinse the olives thoroughly under cold running water, drain them, and pat dry with paper towels. Transfer olives to a large jar or other sealable container and pour in the warm oil along with its seasonings. Cover and leave to marinate overnight on the countertop. Thereafter store in the refrigerator for up to 2 months; remove at least 1 hour before serving to allow the oil to liquefy.

Substitution: Any top-quality plump brined green olive can stand in for the Cerignolas.

Peperoni Ripieni della Nonna
Stuffed Cherry Peppers

The cherry pepper packs a splendid wallop of heat. Preserving it in oil mellows that slightly, and this stuffing of olives, anchovies, and capers makes each a magnificently assertive burst of flavour. It works very well on a platter of salumi. **Makes 24 peppers**

24 fresh cherry peppers
Salt
1½ cups (375 mL) white vinegar
24 large or 48 small anchovy fillets, drained, rinsed, and patted dry
½ cup (125 mL) chopped and pitted brined green olives
¼ cup (60 mL) capers, rinsed and drained
2 cloves garlic, minced
3 cloves garlic, sliced
3 bay leaves
3 sprigs mint
4 sprigs oregano
2 cups (500 mL) grapeseed oil

GARNISH
4 oz (125 g) mozzarella di bufala (optional)
Salt and pepper
Chopped parsley

Carefully trim the peaks from the bottoms of the cherry peppers so that they will sit upright on a tray—but without perforating them. Cut around the stalk of each pepper, then remove and discard. Extract and discard the seeds and pith. Arrange the peppers upright on a small baking sheet. Salt their interiors lightly, and then fill them with white vinegar. Refrigerate overnight.

Drain the peppers and rinse them under cold water. Insert 1 large or 2 small anchovy fillets into each pepper, arranging them in a spiral around the inside wall. In a bowl, combine the olives, capers, and minced garlic. Fill each pepper with the mixture. Stack the stuffed peppers upright, 4 to each layer, in a 1-quart (1 L) Mason jar. Add the sliced garlic, bay leaves, mint, and oregano. Fill the jar with oil to cover. Screw on the lid and refrigerate for at least 2 weeks. The peppers keep for 2 months.

Before serving, insert a small piece of mozzarella di bufala into each pepper, if you choose. Then season and sprinkle with parsley.

Tips: We recommend grapeseed oil for filling the jar because, unlike olive and many other oils, it will not coagulate in the refrigerator. Cherry peppers are generally available fresh for only a few weeks in the autumn.

Arancini
Crisp-Fried Risotto Balls

Once chilled, leftover risotto cannot be reheated, for it turns into an unpalatable, starchy mush. That fact seems sad and unfair only to those who have never enjoyed *arancini*—such a perfect concoction that you might well consider making a small batch of risotto expressly for this otherwise corollary purpose. **Makes 12** *arancini*

3 cups (750 mL) leftover risotto (pages 144–161)
4 oz (125 g) mozzarella di bufala, cubed
Canola oil for deep-frying
Flour for dredging
2 eggs, lightly beaten
2 cups (500 mL) fresh bread crumbs
Salt and pepper
2 cups (500 mL) warm basic tomato sauce (page 82)

Moisten your hands under cold running water and shake them dry. Place a lump of about ¼ cup (60 mL) risotto in the palm of one hand and flatten it. Insert a cube of mozzarella at its centre, fold the sticky rice around it, and roll it between your hands to form a ball with the cheese at its core. Repeat, remoistening your hands as necessary, until all the risotto has been used (yielding about 12 balls).

Pour oil into a cast-iron skillet to a depth of about 1 inch (2.5 cm). Heat to 360°F (185°C).

Meanwhile, in 3 shallow dishes, season the flour, eggs, and bread crumbs with salt and pepper. Dredge the risotto balls in the flour, shaking off the excess. Turn to coat in the egg, and then roll to cover in the bread crumbs. Working in batches if necessary, add them to the hot oil. Fry until golden and crisp on one side, then turn and repeat, about 4 minutes total. With tongs or a slotted spoon, remove *arancini* to drain briefly on a bed of paper towels. Season, and serve with warm tomato sauce for dipping.

Tip: Risotto makes superior *arancini* after it has spent at least a day in the refrigerator. So if you make a fresh batch for the express purpose of making *arancini*, do so ahead of time. Whether using leftover risotto or making a fresh batch, keep in mind that some of the flavours in this book work better for the purpose than others. Mushrooms and truffle, braised duck with olives, and veal marrow all work nicely. But mixed seafood, and flaked salmon with asparagus, not so much.

Sarde in Saor con Pinoli
Cured Sardines with Pine Nuts

The sardine is a hugely underappreciated fish in North America, which is a shame, because they are plentiful, affordable, and healthful and have splendid flavour and texture when treated right. Try this simple, light cure to make converts of your guests at an al fresco summer luncheon. **Serves 6**

12 plump fresh sardines, filleted
2 cups (500 mL) champagne vinegar
½ fennel bulb, julienned
1 small carrot, julienned
1 stalk celery, julienned
5 bay leaves
Salt
1 tbsp (15 mL) dried oregano
1½ cups (375 mL) olive oil
½ cup (125 mL) canola or grapeseed oil

½ cup (125 mL) red wine vinegar
1 tbsp (15 mL) sugar
2 sprigs thyme
½ red onion, julienned
¼ cup (60 mL) toasted pine nuts
2 tbsp (30 mL) chopped parsley
2 tbsp (30 mL) chopped celery leaves
2 tbsp (30 mL) aged wine vinegar
Freshly cracked pepper

Place the fish fillets in a container that will accommodate them snugly in a single layer, then pour over enough champagne vinegar to cover. Cover and refrigerate for 30 minutes.

Scatter half the fennel, carrot, celery, and 2 bay leaves over the bottom of a second container of similar size. Remove the sardines from the vinegar, salt them lightly, and arrange them skin side up on top of the vegetables. Sprinkle with the oregano, and then top with the remaining fennel, carrot, celery, and 2 bay leaves. Stir together the olive and canola oils and pour slowly over the vegetables. Cover and refrigerate for at least 2 hours or overnight.

Meanwhile, in a saucepan, bring the red wine vinegar, sugar, thyme, and remaining bay leaf to a simmer, stirring until the sugar is dissolved. Add the onion and simmer until it begins to soften, about 10 minutes. Set aside to cool.

Arrange 4 sardine fillets on each of 6 chilled plates. Scatter the vegetables over and around the fish. Add a portion of the pickled red onion, and garnish with the pine nuts, parsley, and celery. Drizzle 1 tbsp (15 mL) of the aromatic oil from the marinade over each plate, and finish with 1 tsp (5 mL) aged vinegar and some freshly cracked pepper. (Or serve the sardines on a platter, garnishing as above and dressing the plate with 2 parts oil to 1 part vinegar.)

Tip: The flavour of olive oil is very much desired here, but when pure, it will solidify in the refrigerator. Mixing it instead with canola or grapeseed oil gives you most of the flavour without coagulation.

Suggested Wine: Prosecco

Fritto Misto di Mare
Mixed Fried Fish

When the batter is crisp and light, and both fish and oil are impeccably fresh, *fritto misto* possesses a universal and nearly unchallenged appeal. Each type of seafood suggested below will crisp and cook in very nearly the same amount of time, but the size of your deep-fryer and the extent of your experience with it may encourage you to work in batches of different types of *fritti* until you get the hang of things. And that's fine, for once your guests have a first taste of what's to come, they will be respectfully patient. **Serves 4**

2 eggs
2 cups (500 mL) rice flour
2 cups (500 mL) ice-cold sparkling mineral water
Canola oil for deep-frying
4 calamari, sliced into ¼-inch (5 mm) rings
8 large shrimp, shelled and deveined
8 sea smelts, cleaned, heads removed
4 large sea scallops, halved crosswise
Salt and pepper
2 lemons, halved and charred
1 cup (250 mL) lemon-caper aïoli (page 273)

In a bowl, combine the eggs, flour, and mineral water; whisk together vigorously. Set aside in the refrigerator for 20 minutes.

Heat the oil in a deep-fryer (or in a deep cast-iron skillet) to 360°F (185°C).

Whisk the batter briefly. Working in batches if necessary, dredge the fish and seafood through it, shaking off the excess before carefully transferring them to the deep-fryer. Fry, turning if necessary, until they are golden and crisp, 3 to 4 minutes. Remove with a slotted spoon to drain briefly on a bed of paper towels. Season generously, and serve with charred lemon and a ramekin of aïoli for dipping.

Tip: Larger *fritti*, like the smelts, should be lowered gently by the tail into the hot oil, for the batter will then take on air bubbles that, once you let go, will prevent the fish from sinking in the oil and sticking to the bottom of the pan.

Substitutions: Most fish respond well to being fried. Larger fish, like cod, haddock or even halibut, can be cut into bite-sized pieces and used just like the smelt.

Suggested Wine: Vermentino

Carpaccio di Manzo
Beef Carpaccio

Beef carpaccio was invented in 1950 at Harry's Bar in Venice to commemorate that year's great exhibition of the works of Vittore Carpaccio, the Venetian painter celebrated for, among other things, his exuberant use of red and white. Our take brings a lot of new colour to the dish, but remains faithful in flavour to the original concept. **Serves 4**

1 lb (500 g) top-quality beef tenderloin
1 tbsp (15 mL) olive oil
Sea salt
1 batch carpaccio aïoli (page 273)
4 tsp (20 mL) finely diced onion
4 tsp (20 mL) brined capers, rinsed, drained, and patted dry
4 small radishes, sliced very thinly on a mandoline
¼ cup (60 mL) celery leaves
2 tbsp (30 mL) chopped parsley
¼ cup (60 mL) Piave shavings
½ cup (125 mL) baby arugula, stems trimmed
1 tsp (5 mL) cracked black pepper
Fine olive oil

Heat a dry cast-iron skillet on high heat for about 20 minutes. Rub the tenderloin with the olive oil and sprinkle it with salt on all sides. Salt the skillet. Add the tenderloin to the dry pan and sear it briefly on all sides. Transfer the beef to a rack to cool, then wrap it tightly in plastic wrap and place it in the freezer until it begins to stiffen, about 1 hour. Unwrap the tenderloin, trim the end to straighten it, and use an electric slicer or your sharpest knife to cut it into the thinnest possible discs.

Divide the slices of beef among 4 chilled plates, arranging them so that they overlap and the plate is blanketed with an uninterrupted and virtually translucent layer of raw beef. Drizzle the beef with the thin aïoli, painting white lines in a rough grid. Scatter 1 tsp (5 mL) of onion over each plate, and then do the same with the capers. Follow with the radish discs, then top with the celery leaves, parsley, and Piave. Finish each serving with a scattering of arugula, black pepper, and a generous drizzle of olive oil.

Substitutions: In place of the Piave, you may use another, sharp hard cheese, like the more conventional Parmigiano-Reggiano, or a Caciocavallo Siciliano (but not caciocavallo from the mainland, for these do meet the sharpness criteria).

Tip: If you use a knife instead of a slicer, you may wish to gently pound the discs of meat to render them thinner.

Suggested Wine: Valpolicella or Dolcetto

Polenta

Many people today know polenta only as a semi-gelatinous solid, vacuum-packed into a plastic tube, from which a slice can be cut and transferred directly onto the grill, or a scoop or two melted in a saucepan, making the journey from raw form to the plate in two minutes flat. But that is instant polenta, and it is a product to be ignored. What you want is real polenta in the form Italians have been using since the mid-seventeenth century, when the Venetians brought cornmeal home from America and inspired their countrymen to use it for their creamy porridge in place of the pearl barley and chestnut flour that had come before.

Ideally, the cornmeal should be stone ground, for a little coarseness lends the final product appealing body. Its creaminess comes from gentle heat applied over time, as the cornmeal cooks and grows tender as it absorbs its cooking liquid, bubbling lazily and emitting puffs of steam like some benign sort of lava. Once cooked, the fragrant, creamy, and mildly sweet mixture acquires majesty through the addition of butter and Parmigiano-Reggiano. And with that it becomes an ideal accompaniment to innumerable grilled or braised meats— anything, in short, that you previously thought tasted good with mashed potatoes will shine in this similar company.

Polenta con Code di Maiale Fritte
Creamy Polenta with Crispy Pigs' Tails

As the iconic chef Fergus Henderson put it in his seminal cookbook, *The Whole Beast*, pigs' tails offer the ultimate lip-smacking combination of meat and fat in a package as handily accessible as ice cream on a stick. They also work magnificently with creamy polenta.

Serves 6

6 long pigs' tails, cut into 3 or 4 pieces each
2 yellow onions, sliced
2 medium carrots, sliced
3 cloves garlic, smashed
½ bunch each thyme, oregano, and parsley
2 quarts (2 L) pork stock (page 286)
Salt and pepper
Canola (or other) oil for deep-frying
1 quart (1 L) *brodo* (page 3)

1 cup (250 mL) top-quality stone-ground cornmeal
2 tbsp (30 mL) butter
6 egg yolks, at room temperature

GARNISH
Crispy-fried parsley (page 278)
Freshly grated ricotta salata (or Pecorino Romano)
Fine olive oil

Preheat oven to 250°F (120°C).

Place the pigs' tails in a Dutch oven with the onions, carrots, garlic, thyme, oregano, and parsley. Add enough pork stock to cover and bring to a boil over medium-high heat. Cover, transfer to the oven, and braise for 2½ hours. The flesh of the pigs' tail should now yield easily when pierced with a small knife. If not, braise for another 30 minutes and test again—and repeat as necessary.

Allow the pigs' tails to cool nearly to room temperature in the braising liquid, and before it becomes gelatinous, use a slotted spoon to remove them to a platter. Pass the braising liquid through a sieve into a saucepan and skim off the fat with a ladle. (If you are doing this the day before serving, refrigerate the tails and the liquid separately; the next day, the solidified fat can be easily removed.) Over high heat, reduce the braising liquid by at least three-quarters, until it acquires a viscosity and an intensity adequate for a sauce. Season and keep warm.

Heat the oil in a deep-fryer (or in a deep cast-iron skillet) to 375°F (190°C).

Meanwhile, in a separate saucepan, bring the *brodo* to a vigorous boil. Reduce heat to medium and slowly stir in the cornmeal, about ½ tbsp (7 mL) at a time, stirring continuously—clumps will form if you proceed too quickly. When all the cornmeal has been incorporated, lower heat to a simmer and cook, stirring periodically, until the polenta thickens and begins to pull away from the sides of the pot, about 30 minutes.

When the polenta is almost done, deep-fry the pigs' tails until crisp, about 5 minutes.

Stir the butter into the polenta and season with salt and pepper. Mound ½ cup (125 mL) of the polenta at the centre of each of 6 warm plates. Make a small indentation at the centre of each mound and fill it with an egg yolk. Arrange pieces of pork around it. Drizzle of the pork reduction and garnish with parsley, cheese, and a sprinkle of olive oil.

Substitutions: Chicken, Parmesan, or even vegetable stock can be used in place of the *brodo* for cooking the polenta. Sautéed duck livers or chicken livers work nicely in place of the pigs' tails.

Suggested Wine: Prosecco or Franciacorta

PIZZER

Pizza &

8014601 250315

Cod. Int.

PIZZERIA

DA CONSUMA
ENTRO

Panini

Forno a legna
Wood-Burning Oven

The characteristic domed, fire-brick-lined wood-burning pizza ovens of Naples are the perfect example of how traditional technology can sometimes not be improved upon. Certainly this is so in the eyes of the Associazione Verace Pizza Napoletana, the organization of Neapolitan pizza makers charged with protecting their brand. Their list of rules for what constitutes true Neapolitan pizza pivots on the stipulation that it be prepared exclusively in a wood-burning pizza oven that can cook a pizza in 90 seconds or less at a temperature of at least 800°F (425°C). Their reasoning is not sentimental. In fact, these two criteria are unattainable by an oven powered by any other fuel. No modern gas or electric oven can reach that temperature or cook a pizza in the desired time. Only coal power can match (and surpass) the heat of wood—but its dirty nature makes it unsuitable for the task at hand. Wood does release ash, but the daily sacrifice of a first, undressed pizza at the start of a cooking shift collects it, leaving the stone clean for the pizzas that follow. Their crusts will be thin and soft through the centre and puffy at the edges, where despite their mildly blistered, bronzed surface, they will be foldable without rupture, and the crumb within, aerated and creamy. No other oven can produce these exquisite results.

Neopolitan Pizza

As it was the Neapolitans who in the nineteenth century first thought to dress up traditional flatbread with tomato sauce and cheese—and thus gave us pizza as we know it—it has fallen to them to write the rules of what exactly constitutes a proper pizza pie. And the constitution of the association of Neapolitan pizza makers—the Associazione Verace Pizza Napoletana—is nothing if not precise on the subject.

Their European Union–endorsed stipulations state the following: A Neapolitan pizza should be no more than 35 cm (14 inches) in diameter, with a raised crust of between 1 and 2 cm (½ to ¾ inch) in height, while the balance should not exceed a thickness of 3 mm (¹/₈ inch). This crust must be "soft, elastic, and easily foldable" without cracking. It must be made of "OO" flour, fresh yeast, salt, water, and nothing else, and cooked in a wood-burning oven. Finally, it can be topped only with tomatoes sourced from San Marzano, Italy, as well as either fresh mozzarella di bufala or fior di latte (the cow's milk version of same).

Note that "soft, elastic, and easily foldable" distinguishes Neapolitan pizza from the Roman tradition that later diverged from it with a style of crust that was instead very thin and crisp. And it is those very defining qualities—soft, elastic, foldable—that will prove most elusive when you try to make these recipes at home (unless of course you happen to be equipped with a wood-burning oven). But while they are technically impossible to replicate perfectly in a home oven, with attention to detail and process you can get very respectably close. You might not have a bite, close your eyes, and think that you're in Naples, but you'll be a whole lot closer to it than you are at your local pizza parlour.

Pasta per la Pizza
Pizza Dough

Makes six 12-inch (30 cm) pizzas

2 lb (1 kg) Italian "00" flour
¼ tsp (1 mL) instant dry yeast
2 tbsp (30 mL) kosher salt
All-purpose flour for dusting

Combine the flour and yeast in the bowl of stand mixer with the dough hook attached. Add 2½ cups (625 mL) tepid water and mix on the lowest speed. After 2 minutes, begin slowly adding the salt to the churning dough. Mix for another 10 minutes. The dough should be firm and just a little bit tacky. If the dough is wet and sticky, incorporate a little more flour. If it is dry and hard, incorporate a small amount of water.

On a floured work surface, knead the dough until perfectly smooth, about 5 minutes. Cover with plastic wrap and let rise at room temperature for 1 hour.

Divide the dough into 6 equal portions, and roll each into a ball. Space dough balls out on a lightly floured baking sheet and sprinkle with flour. Cover snugly with a double layer of plastic wrap, then a kitchen cloth, and set aside to rise at room temperature for 6 hours. (The dough can be refrigerated for 3 days, tightly wrapped in plastic. Rest at room temperature for 1 hour before using.)

Place a dough ball on a lightly floured work surface. Begin shaping the ball into a disc by gently pushing outward from its centre with your fingers—as opposed to flattening the ball or exerting any downward pressure on it. Continue pushing and stretching until you have a circle of dough about 6 inches (15 cm) wide and thicker around its edge than across the centre. Now pick it up and drape it over the palm of one hand. Toss it very slowly and gently from one hand to the other, rotating it a little each time and allowing the momentum alone to gently stretch it outward. If the dough is stretching unevenly, place it on the work surface and give it a well-placed nudge or stretch to correct its shape. When the disc of dough is between 12 and 14 inches (30 and 35 cm) wide, place it carefully on the work surface and press down and outward around the perimeter to create a raised ridge of dough to encircle the toppings. Proceed swiftly to dressing the pizza.

Substitutions: The ultra-fine grind of Italian "00"-grade flour is the key to producing this smooth and supple dough and the distinctive creaminess that a good Neapolitan pizza delivers within the crust after being cooked. That said, you can still make acceptable pizza dough with ordinary flour. Try 4½ cups (1.125 L) of all-purpose flour mixed with 1½ cups (375 mL) cake-and-pastry flour for the above recipe, incorporating more all-purpose ¼ cup (60 mL) at a time if it remains tacky after being mixed.

Tip: At Fabbrica we make our pizza dough with fresh yeast. It contributes to a more manageable and consistent dough. If you can procure it, use 2 grams in place of the instant yeast. Dissolve it in a little of the tepid water and proceed as above.

San Marzano Tomatoes

Culinary consensus has it that there is no tomato anywhere on earth better suited to producing sauce than those grown in the soft, mineral-rich volcanic soil of the plains that surround San Marzano, in Campania, where for the tomato plant the weather is most salubrious, too. One of its primary qualities—its thin, easily peeled skin—has also contributed to its mystique, for it makes the fruit too delicate to be mechanically harvested, and they must necessarily be gathered by hand. In 1996, the San Marzano tomato became the only such fruit to be protected by an EU-sanctioned regional certification, a *Denominazione di Origine Protetta*. Taken together, these virtues make this tomato the most expensive variety that you will ever find occupying a can at your local supermarket.

If you pay that price, do not squander the bounty. Understand certain rules. In making a marinara or other basic tomato sauce, tomatoes are cooked to reduce their acidity and increase their sweetness. For pizza, they are used raw because that uncompromised acidity is needed to offset the dough and cheese. In either case, the sauces should never be puréed in a blender or food processor, for their blades will crush seeds and render the sauces bitter. If you are willing to buy San Marzano tomatoes, you should be willing to invest in a food mill, too.

Basic Tomato Sauce

Makes about 3 cups (750 mL)

2 tbsp (30 mL) olive oil
½ medium Spanish onion, sliced
4 cloves garlic, sliced
1 can (28 oz/796 mL) San Marzano tomatoes
Leaves from 1 bunch basil
1 tsp (5 mL) cracked black pepper
Salt

Sweat the onions in the oil until wilted. Add the garlic and sweat for another 3 minutes. Add the tomatoes, half the basil, and the pepper; cover and simmer for 60 minutes. Pass through a food mill fitted with a medium disc into a clean pot. Return to a simmer and add the remaining basil and salt to taste.

Heirloom Tomato Sauce

Makes about 3 cups (750 mL)

3 lb (1.5 kg) heirloom tomatoes, very ripe—but never mealy
3 tbsp (50 mL) olive oil
½ cup (125 mL) minced onion
1 tsp (5 mL) minced garlic
½ cup (125 mL) white wine
2 cups (500 mL) basil leaves, torn
Salt and pepper

Blanch the tomatoes for 60 seconds, shock them in ice water, and then peel. Quarter them, then remove and discard their cores and seeds. Set aside. In a sauté pan over medium heat, sweat the onion in the olive oil until it becomes translucent. Add the garlic, and a minute later deglaze with the white wine. When the wine is reduced to virtually nothing, add the tomatoes. Simmer for no more than 7 minutes, breaking their flesh apart with a wooden spoon as they cook. Add the basil and season lightly.

Tomato Sauce for Pizza

Makes about 3 cups (750 mL)

1 can (28 oz/796 mL) San Marzano tomatoes
2 tsp (10 mL) kosher salt

Remove ½ cup (125 mL) juice from the can. Pass the balance through a food mill fitted with a medium disc. Stir in the salt.

Tip: If you do not have a food mill, it is far better to crush the tomatoes by hand than to pass them through a blender or food processor, both of which will introduce undesired air to the mixture, as well as crushing the seeds and in the process, rendering the mix bitter.

Tomato Passato

Makes about 1 cup (250 mL)

12 Roma tomatoes, halved and seeded
1 tbsp (15 mL) olive oil
1 tbsp (15 mL) combined minced parsley, rosemary, and thyme
Salt and pepper

Preheat oven to 175°F (80°C).

Arrange the tomatoes cut side up and well spaced out on a rack on a baking sheet. Sprinkle with the olive oil, herbs, and salt and pepper. Bake for 12 hours. Peel the tomatoes, transfer to a food processor and buzz briefly—a textured purée is more appealing than a completely smooth one.

Pizza Margherita
Pizza with Tomato, Basil, and Mozzarella

Every pizza enthusiast knows the story of how in the late nineteenth century, a Neapolitan chef named Rafaelle Esposito was seized by a culinary epiphany while seeking to commemorate a visit from Queen Margherita, and invented a pizza just for her using the colours of the new national flag. But while its combination of red, white, and green makes a great story, the enduring magic of the Margherita pizza actually resides in its perfect interplay of flavours. **Makes one 12-inch (30 cm) pizza**

Flour for dusting
1 portion pizza dough, stretched as described on page 76
⅓ cup (75 mL) tomato sauce for pizza (page 83)
5 large basil leaves
3 oz (90 g) mozzarella di bufala, sliced ¼ inch (5 mm) thick
Fine olive oil

Place a pizza stone on the bottom shelf of the oven and preheat to 550°F (290°C) or the highest available setting. Let the stone heat for an additional 30 minutes after the oven has reached its set temperature.

Place the pizza dough on a very lightly floured pizza paddle. Spread the tomato sauce in a thin layer over the pizza dough, stopping about 1 inch (2.5 cm) shy of the edge. Scatter the basil evenly over the tomato sauce, and then distribute the mozzarella over top. Carefully slide the pizza from the paddle onto the hot stone. Shut the oven door as swiftly as possible to minimize heat loss. If convection is available on the oven, activate it. The pizza is done when the edge is risen and thoroughly bronzed, about 5 minutes. Use the paddle to remove the pizza to a cutting board. Sprinkle with olive oil and serve.

Suggested Wine: Chianti

Pizza ai Quattro Formaggi
Pizza with Four Cheeses

A blend of four cheeses is as enticing and comforting a sauce when spread on pizza as it is folded into pasta—and maybe even more so. We build our version of this classic pizza with four assertively distinct Italian cheeses for an exceptionally flavoursome result. But feel free to substitute other cheese of quality. **Makes one 12-inch (30 cm) pizza**

Flour for dusting
1 portion pizza dough, stretched as described on page 76
⅓ cup (75 mL) tomato sauce for pizza (page 83)
5 large basil leaves
3 tbsp (50 mL) shredded Parmigiano-Reggiano (or Grana Padano)
3 tbsp (50 mL) shredded Pecorino Romano
3 tbsp (50 mL) shredded caciocavallo
3 oz (90 g) mozzarella di bufala, sliced ¼ inch (5 mm) thick

Place a pizza stone on the bottom shelf of the oven and preheat to 550°F (290°C) or the highest available setting. Let the stone heat for an additional 30 minutes after the oven has reached its set temperature.

Place the pizza dough on a very lightly floured pizza paddle. Spread the tomato sauce in a thin layer over the pizza dough, stopping about 1 inch (2.5 cm) shy of the edge. Scatter the basil evenly over the tomato sauce, follow with the shredded cheeses, and finish with the sliced mozzarella. Carefully slide the pizza from the paddle onto the hot stone. Shut the oven door as swiftly as possible to minimize heat loss. If convection is available on the oven, activate it. The pizza is done when the crust around the edge is risen and thoroughly bronzed, about 5 minutes. Use the paddle to remove the pizza to a cutting board. Allow to cool and set slightly before cutting and serving.

Substitutions: Feel free to fiddle with the cheese formula according to what is available at the cheesemonger—or in your refrigerator. But try to stay faithful to the formula: for example, the mozzarella should be replaced only with another mild, young cheese, the caciocavallo with another sharp one, and so on.

Suggested Wine: Chianti or Barbera

Pizza alla Salsiccia d'Agnello e Finocchio
Pizza with Lamb Sausage and Fennel

Braised lamb and fennel are a natural pairing. Here they walk together frond in hoof on a pizza garnished with mildly acidic tomato sauce and topped with melted mozzarella. The sum of the parts is exquisite. **Makes one 12-inch (30 cm) pizza**

2 tbsp (30 mL) olive oil
½ cup (125 mL) diced fennel
2 tbsp (30 mL) white wine
1 small lamb sausage (page 279), casing removed
Flour for dusting
1 portion pizza dough, stretched as described on page 76
⅓ cup (75 mL) tomato sauce for pizza (page 83)
5 large basil leaves
3 oz (90 g) mozzarella di bufala, sliced ¼ inch (5 mm) thick
Fine olive oil

Place a pizza stone on the bottom shelf of the oven and preheat to 550°F (290°C) or the highest available setting. Let the stone heat for an additional 30 minutes after the oven has reached its set temperature.

Meanwhile, in a skillet over medium heat, cook the fennel in 1 tbsp (15 mL) of the olive oil until wilted and lightly browned. Deglaze with the wine, then scrape the fennel into a bowl. Return the skillet to the heat and add the remaining olive oil. Sauté the sausage meat until lightly coloured, and then set aside.

Place the pizza dough on a very lightly floured pizza paddle. Spread the tomato sauce in a thin layer over the pizza dough, stopping about 1 inch (2.5 cm) shy of the edge. Scatter the basil evenly over the tomato sauce, and then follow with the sausage meat, fennel, and mozzarella. Carefully slide the pizza from the paddle onto the hot stone. Shut the oven door as swiftly as possible to minimize heat loss. If convection is available on the oven, activate it. The pizza is done when the crust around the edge is risen and thoroughly bronzed, about 5 minutes. Use the paddle to remove the pizza to a cutting board. Sprinkle with olive oil and serve.

Substitution: If you do not wish to make lamb sausage, you may of course use a regular, store-bought one. But use only half a sausage per pizza instead of a whole—the links in our recipe are smaller than usual.

Suggested Wine: Tuscan IGT

Pizza ai Funghi
Pizza with Wild Mushrooms and Truffle Cream

For the mushroom lover, this pizza is bliss. Any wild mushrooms of quality are suitable, but the porcini is ideal. Whatever mushroom or blend of mushrooms you use, the truffle cream will elevate the mix, and the sprinkling of truffle oil on the hot, cooked pizza serves as the *coup de grâce*. **Makes one 12-inch (30 cm) pizza**

½ tbsp (7 mL) olive oil
¾ cup (175 mL) mixed top-quality whole mushrooms (porcini, chanterelles, blue foot, etc.)
Salt and pepper
1 tbsp (15 mL) truffle paste
⅓ cup (75 mL) *besciamella* (page 275), at room temperature
Flour for dusting
1 portion pizza dough, stretched as described on page 76
3 oz (90 g) mozzarella di bufala, sliced ¼ inch (5 mm) thick
Truffle oil (optional)

Place a pizza stone on the bottom shelf of the oven and preheat to 550°F (290°C) or the highest available setting. Let the stone heat for an additional 30 minutes after the oven has reached its set temperature.

Cook the mushrooms in the olive oil over medium heat until they wilt and release their liquid. Season, and then use a slotted spoon to remove them to a cutting board, reserving the juices in the pan. Slice any that are too large to be comfortably managed in a mouthful, and set aside.

Place the pizza dough on a very lightly floured pizza paddle. Stir the truffle paste and the mushroom juices into the *besciamella*. Spread the *besciamella* in a thin layer over the pizza dough, stopping about 1 inch (2.5 cm) shy of the edge. Distribute the mushrooms evenly over top, and follow with the mozzarella. Carefully slide the pizza from the paddle onto the hot stone. Shut the oven door as swiftly as possible to minimize heat loss. If convection is available on the oven, activate it. The pizza is done when the crust around the edge is risen and thoroughly bronzed, about 5 minutes. Use the paddle to remove the pizza to a cutting board. Sprinkle with truffle oil, if you choose, and serve.

Suggested Wine: Chianti or Barbaresco

Pizza al Capocollo, Pomodoro e Basilico
Pizza with Spicy Capocollo, Tomato, and Basil

The artisanal capocollo we serve at Fabbrica is aged in our meat locker for a minimum of four months. Hopefully you can find one that is nearly as good. If you do, treat it gently, and remember that it does not like heat. Our pizza oven hovers around 900°F and cooks a pie in less than 2 minutes, and the capocollo survives the ordeal unscathed, but the longer cooking time in a home oven will toughen it and drive out its fat. We recommend adding the sausage just long enough before the pizza is done to heat it through and leave it softened.

Makes one 12-inch (30 cm) pizza

Flour for dusting
1 portion pizza dough, stretched as described on page 76
⅓ cup (75 mL) tomato sauce for pizza (page 83)
5 large basil leaves
3 oz (90 g) mozzarella di bufala, sliced ¼ inch (5 mm) thick
6 thin slices top-quality spicy capocollo
Fine olive oil

Place a pizza stone on the bottom shelf of the oven and preheat to 550°F (290°C) or the highest available setting. Let the stone heat for an additional 30 minutes after the oven has reached its set temperature.

Place the pizza dough on a very lightly floured pizza paddle. Spread the tomato sauce in a thin layer over the pizza dough, stopping about 1 inch (2.5 cm) shy of the edge. Scatter the basil evenly over the tomato sauce, and then distribute the mozzarella over top. Carefully slide the pizza from the paddle onto the hot stone. Shut the oven door as swiftly as possible to minimize heat loss. If convection is available on your oven, activate it. When the crust is lightly bronzed and appears to be about 1 minute from done, open the oven door, slide out the pizza stone, and quickly distribute the capocollo over the pizza before returning it to the oven to finish cooking. Use the paddle to remove the pizza to a cutting board. Sprinkle with olive oil and serve.

Suggested Wine: Gavi or Valpolicella

Pizza al Prosciutto e Rucola
Pizza with Prosciutto and Arugula

For this recipe, seek out the best possible prosciutto—and the longest-aged joint available—for in addition to the benefits of flavour, pleasurable chewing of the pizza hinges on prosciutto that surrenders obligingly to advancing teeth. The spicy and refreshing bite of arugula serves as a perfect counterpoint to this majestic ham.

Makes one 12-inch (30 cm) pizza

Flour for dusting
1 portion pizza dough, stretched as described on page 76
⅓ cup (75 mL) tomato sauce for pizza (page 83)
5 large basil leaves
3 oz (90 g) mozzarella di bufala, sliced ¼ inch (5 mm) thick
4 thin slices well-aged prosciutto di Parma (or other top-quality cured ham)
1 large handful peppery baby arugula, stems trimmed
Fine olive oil
Cracked pepper

Place a pizza stone on the bottom shelf of the oven and preheat to 550°F (290°C) or the highest available setting. Let the stone heat for an additional 30 minutes after the oven has reached its set temperature.

Place the pizza dough on a very lightly floured pizza paddle. Spread the tomato sauce in a thin layer over the pizza dough, stopping about 1 inch (2.5 cm) shy of the edge. Scatter the basil evenly over the tomato sauce, and then distribute the mozzarella over top. Carefully slide the pizza from the paddle onto the hot stone. Shut the oven door as swiftly as possible to minimize heat loss. If convection is available on the oven, activate it. When the crust around the edge is risen and completely bronzed, use the paddle to remove the pizza to a cutting board. Arrange the prosciutto one slice per quadrant in a rumpled cross, scatter the pizza with arugula, sprinkle with olive oil and cracked pepper, and serve.

Suggested Wine: Valpolicella

Pizza ai Frutti di Mare
Pizza with Clams and Shrimp

Fragrant pesto diluted with olive oil makes a perfect backdrop for the intermingling flavours of salty clams and sweet shrimp. Makes one 12-inch (30 cm) pizza

3 tbsp (50 mL) olive oil
1 clove garlic, smashed
4 medium shrimp, shelled, deveined, and split lengthwise
Salt and pepper
12 clams
¼ cup (60 mL) white wine

2 tbsp (30 mL) basil pesto (page 281)
Flour for dusting
1 portion pizza dough, stretched as described on page 76
2 oz (60 g) mozzarella di bufala, sliced
Fine olive oil

Place a pizza stone on the bottom shelf of the oven and preheat to 550°F (290°C) or the highest available setting. Let the stone heat for an additional 30 minutes after the oven has reached its set temperature.

In a sauté pan, sauté the garlic in 2 tbsp (30 mL) of the olive oil until it is lightly coloured. Add the shrimp, season, and sauté lightly—do not cook them all the way through. Remove the shrimp to a plate. Add the clams to the sauté pan and cook for 1 minute. Add the white wine, bring to a boil, cover, and lower the heat. Remove the clams as they pop open. (Discard any that do not.) Shuck, and reserve the clam meat.

Place the pizza dough on a very lightly floured pizza paddle. Thin the pesto with the remaining 1 tbsp (15 mL) olive oil, and then spread the mixture in a thin layer over the pizza dough, stopping about 1 inch (2.5 cm) shy of the edge. Scatter with the mozzarella. Carefully slide the pizza from the paddle onto the hot stone. Shut the oven door as swiftly as possible to minimize heat loss. If convection is available on the oven, activate it. When the crust of the pizza has risen and is just beginning to acquire colour, open the oven door, slide out the pizza stone, and quickly distribute the shrimp and clams over the pizza before returning it to the oven to finish cooking. Two or 3 minutes later, when the crust around the edge is thoroughly bronzed, use the paddle to remove the pizza to a cutting board. Sprinkle with fine olive oil and serve.

Substitutions: Fresh buffalo ricotta also works nicely with the seafood and pesto. You may dab the pizza with it along with mozzarella at the start, or you may choose to use fresh ricotta exclusively. In lieu of your finest olive oil, flavoured oil left over from Marinated Cerignola Olives (page 55) works beautifully when drizzled on this pizza.

Suggested Wine: Soave

Panino Caprese
Tomato and Buffalo Mozzarella

Here, the classic caprese salad is seamlessly transplanted to a new residence between two slices of crisp focaccia. It works especially well because the unreliable tomato component is reliably intensified with a long stint in a low-temperature oven. **Makes 4 panini**

8 slices focaccia, about ½ inch (1 cm) thick
½ cup (125 mL) butter, softened
2 large balls mozzarella di bufala (each about 7 oz/200 g), sliced ¼ inch (5 mm) thick
8 Roma tomatoes, halved, dried, and peeled (see page 83)
32 leaves crispy-fried sage (page 278)
Salt and pepper

Preheat oven to 350°F (180°C).

Generously butter one side of each slice of the focaccia, and then fry, buttered side down, in a nonstick skillet until the bottom is bronzed and crisp. Arrange 4 slices on a baking sheet, toasted side down. Top each slice with 4 slices of mozzarella. Top that with 4 tomato halves and 8 leaves of crispy sage. Finish with a second slice of focaccia, toasted side up, and transfer to the oven until heated through, about 5 minutes. Slice in half on the diagonal and serve.

Variation: Like all sandwiches in this section, the Caprese also works nicely heated in a panini press instead of the oven. This panino is a lovely vegetarian sandwich, but some might consider it to be improved with the addition of some crisp pancetta (page 278). Add 3 slices to each sandwich.

Panino Pasquale
Grilled Chicken with Zucchini Relish

At first glance this sandwich may appear to be excessively labour-intensive. Maybe it is. But anyone who has tasted it will attest that the effort is well worth it. Do give it a try.

Makes 4 panini

2 boneless, skinless chicken breasts
   (about 1 lb/500 g total)
½ cup (125 mL) Roasted Garlic Dressing (page 27)
¼ cup (60 mL) olive oil
1 small yellow onion, diced
1 medium yellow zucchini
1 medium green zucchini
Salt and pepper

½ cup (125 mL) chopped oil-preserved cubanelle peppers
¼ cup (60 mL) butter
½ tbsp (7 mL) white balsamic vinegar
8 slices focaccia, about ½ inch (1 cm) thick
1 large ball mozzarella di bufala (about 7 oz/200 g),
   sliced ¼ inch (5 mm) thick
12 slices crisp pancetta (page 278)
⅓ cup (75 mL) cured tomato aïoli (page 273)

Butterfly each chicken breast, place them between 2 sheets of plastic wrap, and pound them to a thickness of about ¼ inch (5 mm). Cut each breast in half, transfer to a sealable container, and add the Roasted Garlic Dressing. Turn the chicken to coat it well, cover, and transfer to the refrigerator to marinate for at least 2 hours.

Preheat grill on high.

Cook the onion over medium heat in 1 tbsp (15 mL) of the olive oil until lightly caramelized; set aside to cool. Slice the zucchini lengthwise about ¼ inch (5 mm) thick. Brush lightly with olive oil, season, and then char on the grill. Arrange the grilled zucchini on a platter in a single layer, then transfer to the freezer for 5 minutes to arrest their cooking. Pulse the cooled zucchini in a food processor until chunky, and then transfer to a cheese-cloth-lined strainer placed over a bowl. Cover with plastic wrap and let drain for at least 2 hours. In a bowl, combine the drained zucchini with the chopped peppers and caramelized onion. Mix well, taste, adjust seasonings, and set aside in the refrigerator until needed.

Preheat grill on high again, and preheat oven to 375°F (190°C).

In a small saucepan, melt the butter on low heat, stir in the balsamic vinegar, and set aside. Brush one side of each focaccia slice with olive oil, season, and grill the slices oiled side down, rotating once to make cross-hatch marks. Transfer the bread to a baking sheet, grilled side down. Grill the chicken for about 2 minutes per side. Meanwhile, brush the top of each focaccia slice with the balsamic butter and transfer the baking sheet to the oven for 5 minutes.

To assemble, arrange 4 slices of focaccia grilled side down. Spread each with about 2 tbsp (30 mL) of the zucchini relish. Top with half a chicken breast, 3 or 4 slices of mozzarella, and 3 slices of pancetta. Smear the remaining focaccia slices with about 4 tsp (20 mL) tomato aïoli and cover the sandwiches with the top halves.

Substitution: You may use oil-preserved peperoncini in place of the cubanelle peppers, but as they are considerably spicier, use fewer—about 4 tsp (20 mL) should suffice.

Shortcut: Omit the balsamic butter and simply oil and grill both sides of the bread.

Panino Mimmo
Prosciutto, Roast Peppers, and Smoked Provolone

Like so many Italian dishes, the excellence of this sandwich relies on the quality of its constituent parts. Stringy prosciutto will ruin it—so use only the finest, best-aged prosciutto di Parma that you can find. Likewise, buy a quality Italian provolone. **Serves 4**

4 pieces ciabatta, each about 5 by 4 inches (12 by 10 cm), split
½ cup (125 mL) antipasto spread (page 274)
1 cup (250 mL) roasted garlic peppers (page 282)
12 slices top-quality prosciutto
8 slices smoked provolone

Spread 1 tbsp (15 mL) of antipasto spread on the cut side of each piece of ciabatta. Dress each of the bottom halves with ¼ cup (60 mL) of the peppers, 3 slices of prosciutto, and 2 slices of provolone. Cover with the top halves and grill in a panini press until bronzed and crisp. Slice in half on the diagonal before serving.

Substitutions: Calabrese is as nice a fit as the ciabatta. The provolone need not be smoked.

Panino Dante
Mushrooms, Apple, Watercress, and Gorgonzola

Crisp, tart apple is a classic accompaniment for pungent blue cheese. So are sautéed mushrooms—especially when the blue cheese is gorgonzola, transformed into a creamy spread. Here they commingle, along with some spicy watercress, between two crisp slices of bread to make a sandwich that seems far too satisfying to be vegetarian.

Makes 4 panini

¾ cup (175 mL) mascarpone, at room temperature
2 oz (60 g) gorgonzola, at room temperature
1 tbsp (15 mL) olive oil
3 cups (750 mL) mixed top-quality mushrooms
Salt and pepper
¼ tsp (1 mL) minced rosemary
1 tsp (5 mL) lemon juice
8 slices focaccia, about ½ inch (1 cm) thick
½ cup (125 mL) butter, softened
1 Granny Smith apple, cored and julienned
1 cup (250 mL) loosely packed watercress leaves
1 tbsp (15 mL) fine olive oil

Blend the mascarpone and gorgonzola with a fork until smooth, and set aside. Sauté the mushrooms in the olive oil until wilted. Season, stir in the rosemary, and deglaze with half the lemon juice. Remove from the heat and set aside.

Butter the focaccia on one side. Heat a large nonstick pan on medium-low. Working in batches, fry the focaccia slices, buttered side down, until crisp and golden. Arrange the bread, toasted side down, on a work surface. Spread 4 tsp (20 mL) of the gorgonzola mixture on each slice.

In a bowl, combine the apple and watercress. Add the olive oil and the remaining ½ tsp (2 mL) lemon juice, season, and toss well. Divide the mushrooms among the 4 focaccia slices. Mound the watercress and apple mixture on top of the mushrooms. Slice the sandwiches in half on the diagonal and serve.

Panino Sergio
Meatloaf

Poaching the meatloaf in *brodo* makes for an exceptionally tender result. Dressed with our excellent tomato sauce and fresh buffalo mozzarella, and wrapped in a quality calabrese with crisp crust and a light, airy crumb, this is our ultimate meatloaf sandwich. **Serves 10**

4 tsp (20 mL) olive oil
1 yellow onion, minced
1 tsp (5 mL) minced garlic
1½ cups (375 mL) cubed white bread, crusts removed
2 cups (500 mL) 2% milk
½ lb (250 g) each minced veal, pork, and lean beef
2 eggs
½ cup (125 mL) grated Parmigiano-Reggiano
2 tbsp (30 mL) combined minced oregano, basil, and parsley

½ tsp (2 mL) chili flakes
Salt and pepper
2 quarts (2 L) *brodo* (page 3)
½ cup (125 mL) butter
1 tbsp (15 mL) white balsamic vinegar
1 large calabrese ring loaf (or 2 long loaves)
1 batch basic tomato sauce (page 82)
4 oz (125 g) mozzarella di bufala
Leaves from 1 bunch basil

Sweat the onion in 1 tbsp (15 mL) of the olive oil until wilted, about 5 minutes. Stir in the garlic and sweat for another 2 minutes. Set aside to cool and then chill in the refrigerator.

Meanwhile, place the bread in a bowl, cover with the milk, and let stand for 5 minutes. In a large bowl, combine the veal, pork, beef, and eggs; using your hands or a paddle, work the mixture together thoroughly. Add the Parmesan, minced herbs, and chili flakes. Remove the bread from the milk and squeeze it gently, reserving the milk. Add the bread to the meat mixture and work together for at least 5 minutes. If the mixture is dry and sticky, add some of the reserved milk and mix again. Season lightly and mix again.

Bring the *brodo* to a simmer. Heat a small skillet on medium-high. Remove a meatball-sized sample of the mixture and sear it in the remaining teaspoon (5 mL) olive oil. Taste, and correct seasonings. Shape the mixture into a cylindrical loaf. Place the meatloaf in a fish poacher that will accommodate it without too much extra space. Cover with the hot *brodo*, bring to a boil, then reduce heat to a simmer. Cover and cook until the internal temperature of the meatloaf reaches 170°F (75°C), about 40 minutes. Let the meatloaf cool to room temperature in its poaching liquid.

Preheat oven to 375°F (190°C).

Melt the butter in a small saucepan over low heat, stir in the balsamic vinegar, and set aside. Slice the calabrese horizontally to form 2 rings. Brush the cut side of each half with the balsamic butter. Transfer the bread crust side down to the oven for 5 minutes. Meanwhile, cut the meatloaf into ½-inch (1 cm) slices, place them in a large sauté pan, cover with the tomato sauce, and bring to a simmer. Cut the mozzarella into ¼-inch (5 mm) slices. Place the bottom ring of the bread on a baking sheet, crust down, and dress it with a single layer of mozzarella. Follow with slices of tomato-sauce doused meatloaf, then the basil, and finish with a second layer of mozzarella. Cover with the top ring of bread and transfer to the oven for 5 minutes. Transfer to a platter, slice, and serve with a large ramekin of tomato sauce.

Variation: We concieved this as a party platter. If you wish instead to make individual sandwiches, use focaccia and grill as described on page 100.

Pasta &

Gnocchi

Pasta Dough

Making your own pasta dough is so quick and simple, and the results so pleasing, that once you get the hang of it you'll never turn back.

Basic
Makes about 1 lb (500 g), enough for 4 main-course servings

1½ cups (375 mL) Italian "00" flour
3 eggs
2 tbsp (30 mL) olive oil
1 tsp (5 mL) salt

Sift the flour into the bowl of a stand mixer fitted with the dough hook. Add the eggs and olive oil, turn the mixer onto low speed, and add the salt. Mix on low speed until the dough clumps together in a ball. The dough should feel only vaguely tacky. If it is sticky to the touch, incorporate a little more flour. On a floured work surface, knead the dough for 2 or 3 minutes. Roll it into a ball, wrap it tightly in plastic wrap, and set aside to rest in the refrigerator for at least 30 minutes before rolling. Dust the dough with flour again before passing it through a pasta machine. Add more flour if the pasta sticks to the rollers (pay special attention to this in summer, when humidity is at its highest). After rolling the dough, rest it again for 30 minutes at room temperature before using.

Nero
Makes about 1 lb (500 g), enough for 4 main-course servings

1½ cups (375 mL) semolina flour
2 eggs
4 tsp (20 mL) squid ink
Flour for dusting

Place the semolina flour in a food processor. In a small bowl, combine the eggs, squid ink, and 2 tbsp (30 mL) cold water, and whisk until smooth. Pulse the food processor, adding the liquid at intervals. When the liquid is incorporated, scrape down the sides of the bowl with a rubber spatula, and pulse one more time. The dough should appear dry and crumbly, but feel damp to the touch. Transfer to a flour-dusted work surface and knead for 15 minutes. Roll into a ball, wrap tightly in plastic wrap, and rest at room temperature for at least 30 minutes. (The dough is good for an hour at room temperature or 4 days in the refrigerator, or it can be frozen.) Dust the dough with flour again before passing it through a pasta machine. See the tips above.

Spaghetti al Nero di Seppia con Seppie, Cozze e Zucchine
Squid Ink Pasta with Squid, Mussels, and Zucchini

Needless to say, squid-ink-dyed pasta loves sautéed squid for company. Here we add mussels to the mix, along with sautéed zucchini for colour and chili for heat. For the seafood enthusiast, it is a most enticing mix.

Serves 6 as an appetizer or 4 as a main course

2 cloves garlic
¼ cup (60 mL) olive oil
⅓ cup (75 mL) minced onion
2 lb (1 kg) mussels, scrubbed and debearded
1¾ cups (425 mL) white wine
14 oz (420 g) dry or 20 oz (600 g) fresh
   squid ink pasta (page 108)
2 small squid, cut into ¼-inch (5 mm) rings,
   with their tentacles

1 small zucchini, halved lengthwise, sliced ¼ inch
   (5 mm) thick
2 tbsp (30 mL) puréed tomato passato or tomato paste
½ tsp (2 mL) chili flakes
Salt and pepper
2 tbsp (30 mL) butter
2 tbsp (30 mL) chopped parsley
Squeeze of lemon juice
Fine olive oil

Crush one clove of garlic and mince the other; set aside. In a sauté pan over medium-low heat, sweat 2 tbsp (30 mL) of the onion in 2 tbsp (30 mL) of the olive oil until wilted. Add the crushed garlic and sweat a minute longer. Raise the heat to medium-high. Add the mussels and 1½ cups (325 mL) of the wine. When the wine begins to boil, lower heat to a simmer and cover the pan. Remove mussels as they pop open. (Discard any that do not.) Strain the cooking liquid and reserve ¼ cup (60 mL). Pull mussels from their shells and set aside, covered.

Begin cooking the pasta. Meanwhile, in the same sauté pan, sweat the remaining onion in the remaining olive oil. Once it has wilted, add the minced garlic and sweat a minute longer. Raise the heat to medium. Add the squid and cook, stirring frequently, for 1 minute longer. Add the zucchini and sauté for 1 minute. Stir in the tomato paste, and follow with the remaining wine. Reduce by half, and then add the mussels and their reserved cooking liquid. Once that has heated through, stir in the chili flakes, and season with salt and pepper. When the liquid has reduced by half, stir in the butter, parsley, and lemon juice.

Drain the pasta, reserving ½ cup (125 mL) of the cooking water. Combine the sauce with the pasta over low heat. If it looks dry, add a little of the cooking water. Divide the pasta among warm plates and drizzle each with fine olive oil.

Suggested Wine: Ribolla Gialla or Vernaccia

Linguine alle Vongole, Peperoncino e Vino Bianco
Linguine with Clams, Chili, and White Wine

This classic dish is an ode to simplicity. The small handful of flavours at play work so well together that adding anything new to the mix would detract from instead of enhancing their act. **Serves 6 as an appetizer or 4 as a main course**

14 oz (420 g) dry or 20 oz (600 g) fresh linguine
3 tbsp (50 mL) olive oil
¼ cup (60 mL) minced onion
2 cloves garlic, minced
2 tsp (10 mL) minced oil-preserved red chilies
2 lb (1 kg) littleneck or other quality clams, scrubbed and flushed (see page 7)
¾ cup (175 mL) white wine
2 tbsp (30 mL) butter
Salt and white pepper
2 tbsp (30 mL) minced parsley, plus additional for garnish
Squeeze of lemon juice

Begin cooking the pasta. Meanwhile, in a sauté pan sweat the onion in the olive oil until translucent. Stir in the garlic and chilies; cook a minute longer. Raise heat and add the clams and white wine. After a minute, cover. Remove the clams as they pop open. Discard any that do not. Stir in the butter and adjust seasonings. Shuck some of the clams, if desired.

Drain the pasta, reserving 1 cup (250 mL) of the cooking water. Combine the pasta, sauce, clams, and parsley over low heat. If it looks dry, add a little of the cooking water. Toss well, add lemon juice, and adjust seasonings. Serve topped with more minced parsley.

Suggested Wine: Vermentino or Vernaccia di San Gimignano

Strozzapreti al Ragù Napoletano
Strozzapreti with Neapolitan-Style Pork Ragù

The traditional Bolognese ragù is largely based on beef. The Neapolitan equivalent generally leans more to pork—and our take is a pork extravaganza, featuring four different cuts along with pork stock. It is all the more flavoursome for it. **Serves 8 as a main course**

2 lb (1 kg) pork shoulder
1 lb (500 g) pork belly, from the less fatty end
2 tbsp (30 mL) olive oil
1 medium Spanish onion, chopped
1 pig's foot, split
Salt and pepper
6-oz (170 g) slab prosciutto, halved
¼ bunch parsley
¼ bunch oregano
1 cup (250 mL) white wine

2 cans (each 28 oz/796 mL) San Marzano tomatoes
1 quart (1 L) pork stock (page 286)
28 oz (840 g) dry or 40 oz (1.25 kg) fresh strozzapreti
Leaves from ¼ bunch parsley, chopped
Leaves from ¼ bunch basil, torn
¼ cup (60 mL) butter

GARNISH
¼ cup fine olive oil
Grated Parmigiano-Reggiano or Pecorino Romano

Trim the pork shoulder of excess fat and cut into 3 pieces. Trim the pork belly of skin and excess fat and cut into 1-inch (2.5 cm) cubes.

In a large saucepan over medium-high heat, cook the onions in the oil until lightly caramelized, about 7 minutes. Meanwhile, generously season the shoulder, belly, and foot and add to the pot along with the prosciutto. Cook, turning occasionally, until the meat is browned all over. Add the parsley and oregano and deglaze with the white wine. When that has nearly evaporated, add the tomatoes and stock. Bring to a boil, then lower the heat, season lightly, cover, and simmer for 2 hours.

Discard the prosciutto. Remove the foot and pieces of pork shoulder. Scrape the meat from the inside of the foot; return the meat to the pot and discard the balance. Break up the shoulder meat, discard any gristle or excess fat, and return the meat to the pot. Crush the tomatoes and large pieces of belly with the edge of a wooden spoon, stir well, and adjust seasonings.

Cook the pasta, then drain, reserving 2 cups (500 mL) of the starchy water. Reheat the desired amount of pork ragù. Fold in the parsley, basil, and butter. Combine pasta and sauce over low heat. Add enough starchy water to moisten the sauce, and adjust seasonings. Serve topped with a drizzle of fine olive oil and grated cheese.

Tip: There will be pasta sauce left over. In the unlikely event that you do not wish to use it within the week, it freezes well for up to 3 months.

Suggested Wine: Aglianico or Cannonau di Sardegna

Fettuccine al Granchio e Uova in Camicia
Fettuccine with Crab and Poached Egg

The only mark against crab is the trouble it takes to pick it out of its shell—which is why doing so ahead of time, and serving it with pasta, unfailingly goes over well with guests at the dinner table. Crabmeat is sweet, and it loves the company of cream. Here that union is enriched with the addition of a soft-poached egg. **Serves 4 as a main course**

2 frozen Alaskan King crab legs
2 tbsp (30 mL) olive oil
¼ cup (60 mL) julienned guanciale
¼ cup (60 mL) minced onion
1 clove garlic, minced
¼ cup (60 mL) white wine
1½ cups (375 mL) 35% cream

1 tbsp (15 mL) crab essence (optional; page 286)
14 oz (420 g) dry or 20 oz (600 g) fresh fettuccine
Squeeze of lemon juice
1 tbsp (15 mL) minced parsley
Salt and pepper
4 soft-poached eggs

Soak the crab legs in cold water until thawed. Split the shells with kitchen shears and pull out the meat, picking over it carefully for shell fragments and cartilage. Set aside.

In a skillet on medium heat, sauté the guanciale in the oil until it begins to crisp. Add the onion, stirring frequently until it begins to wilt. Add the garlic and cook 1 minute longer. Deglaze with the white wine. When that has reduced by half, add the cream and, if you choose, the crab essence. Reduce the cream until it coats the back of a spoon.

Meanwhile, cook the pasta. Add the crab to the cream sauce. Drain the pasta, and over low heat, toss with the sauce. Fold in the lemon juice and parsley, season, and toss again. Taste and correct seasonings. Divide among four warm plates, top each portion with a poached egg, and serve.

Substitutions: The Alaskan King crab legs can be replaced with 1 lb (500 g) of any other crabmeat that comes in decent-sized chunks. The compilation also works well all'aragosta—with lobster. Two lobsters of about 1½ lb (750 g) will suffice. You may use pancetta in place of the guanciale. A top-quality bacon will also do in a pinch, but not if it is heavily smoked, which will overpower the sauce.

Suggested Wine: Prosecco or Franciacorta

Tortiglioni al Forno con Polpette
Oven-Baked Tortiglioni with Meatballs

Many North Americans consider spaghetti and meatballs to be the ultimate comfort food, on account of the hearty, satisfying nature of the dish and the likelihood that it was their introduction to pasta as a child. Here we render the Italian American classic even more comforting through the indulgent addition of scads of molten cheese. Serves 6 as a main course

1 batch meatloaf (page 105)
2 tbsp (30 mL) toasted pine nuts
2 tbsp (30 mL) golden raisins, chopped
½ tbsp (7 mL) olive oil
2 batches basic tomato sauce (page 82), at a simmer
1 cup (250 mL) basil leaves, torn
½ cup (125 mL) parsley leaves, chopped
½ cup (125 mL) grated Parmigiano-Reggiano
21 oz (600 g) dry tortiglioni
3 large balls mozzarella di bufala (each about 7 oz/200 g), cubed

Make the meatloaf mixture as described on page 105, including the pine nuts and raisins when you add the Parmesan and herbs. Heat a small skillet on medium-high and add the olive oil. Remove a small sample of the mixture, shape it into a patty, and sear it on both sides. Taste, and correct seasonings if necessary.

Rinse hands under cold running water and begin forming meatballs about 1 inch (2.5 cm) wide, rinsing hands again as necessary whenever the meat gets sticky. Add the meatballs to the tomato sauce and raise heat to medium-high, until the sauce begins to bubble. Lower heat, cover, and simmer for about 25 minutes—until the meatballs are cooked through and firm. With the edge of a wooden spoon break each meatball into two or three pieces, then stir in the basil, parsley, and Parmesan, and set aside.

Preheat oven to 450°F (225°C).

Cook and drain the pasta, reserving 1 cup (250 mL) of the cooking liquid. Fold together the pasta and sauce over low heat. If it seems dry, incorporate some of the pasta water. Correct the seasonings. Stir in about two-thirds of the cubed mozzarella and then transfer mixture to 1 large (or 6 individual) casserole dish(es). Top with remaining cheese. Transfer to the top rack of the oven until cheese is melted, bubbling, and lightly bronzed—about 10 minutes.

Substitutions: Rigatoni is a perfectly good substitute for the recommended tortiglioni.

Suggested Wine: Chianti

Orecchiette con Brasato di Coniglio e Cime di Rapa
Orecchiette with Braised Rabbit and Rapini

The flesh of the farmed North American rabbit does not have the character or depth of its wild counterpart more commonly eaten in Europe. But all the same, when properly braised it is more supple and tender, and here its mild sweetness mixes seductively with the robust flavour and slight bitterness of the rapini and the heat of the chili.

Serves 6 as an appetizer or 4 as a main course

1 rabbit (about 3½ lb/1.6 kg), braised (see page 215)
14 oz (420 g) dry or 20 oz (600 g) fresh orecchiette
3 tbsp (50 mL) olive oil
¼ cup (60 mL) minced onion
2 cloves garlic, minced
2 tsp (10 mL) minced oil-preserved red chilies
¼ cup (60 mL) white wine
2 tbsp (30 mL) butter
Salt and white pepper
1 bunch rapini, stems trimmed, blanched
½ cup (125 mL) grated Pecorino Romano

Cut (or ask your butcher to cut) the rabbit into 7 serving pieces (2 hind legs, 2 forelegs, 2 saddles, and 1 double-rack). Braise the rabbit as described on page 215, but omit the mushrooms and olives. Allow to cool slightly, then remove the rabbit from the braising liquid. Shred the meat from the bone and set aside. Remove the herb sprigs from the braising liquid and blitz the sauce in a blender (or with a hand blender); strain and set aside.

Begin cooking the pasta. Meanwhile, in a sauté pan cook the onion in the olive oil until translucent. Stir in the garlic and chilies; cook a minute longer. Raise the heat and deglaze with the white wine. When that has reduced by half, add the rabbit meat and about 1 quart (1 L) of the sauce; bring to a simmer. Lower the heat, stir in the butter, and season.

Drain the pasta, reserving 1 cup (250 mL) of the cooking water. Combine the pasta, sauce, and rapini over low heat. Toss well and adjust seasonings. If it seems dry, incorporate some of the pasta water, ¼ cup (60 mL) at a time. Serve topped with grated pecorino.

Suggested Wine: Soave or Pinot Nero

Olio d'Oliva Olive Oil

Every region of Italy save for Piedmont and Val d'Aosta produces olive oil, and unsurprisingly, just as with wine, each is celebrated for having different predominant characteristics. The vast majority of Italian olive oil—nearly 80 percent—is produced in the south. These are generally well balanced, and possess a mild, sunny sweetness. In Puglia, olives are harvested extremely late, and sometimes merely shaken from the tree onto sheets on the ground, so the oils extracted from them are heavy and ripe. Tuscan oils are produced from olives grown on hillsides, perpetually in the sun; they taste mellow and nutty, and often peppery in the finish. The oils of Calabria are praised for their almond notes, and those from Liguria are pale, delicate, and sweet. Many consider the oils from Genoa to be the lightest of all. Everyone has a favourite.

The thing to remember is to try is to have a different favourite for different uses and occasions. Cook with a basic, workhorse oil, not with unfiltered extra virgin oils of great quality. These are for finishing dishes, as a final seasoning. They are likewise too assertively flavoured to dress a salad unless diluted with a more basic olive oil. Finally, resist hoarding oil in the cupboard or cellar; in fact, never buy more than you can use over a couple of months. It tastes best fresh and spoils quickly, especially when exposed to sunlight.

Ravioli di Spinaci e Tuorlo al Burro e Tartufo
Spinach and Egg Yolk Ravioli with Butter and Truffle

Eggs, butter, and spinach always play nicely together at Sunday brunch. Here, we give the combination a dinner-table-worthy upgrade by wrapping it up in delicate thin pasta and dressing it up with artisanal butter and shaved truffle. **Serves 6**

1 tbsp (15 mL) olive oil
2 tbsp (30 mL) minced onion
3 bunches baby spinach, stems removed
Salt and pepper
Freshly grated nutmeg
1 batch basic pasta dough (page 108)

6 egg yolks
1 egg, lightly beaten
½ cup (125 mL) artisanal butter, cubed
Truffle shavings
Fine olive oil

Sweat the onion in the olive oil in a large Dutch oven on low heat. When the onion has completely wilted, add the spinach and cover. Cook, stirring periodically, until the spinach has wilted completely. Season with salt, pepper, and nutmeg. Transfer the spinach to a colander or large strainer to drain, pressing down hard on the spinach to drive out the water. Wrap the spinach in paper towels and squeeze. Repeat with fresh paper towels until no more liquid can be extracted. Set aside.

Roll the pasta into thin sheets and spread them out on a floured work surface. Cut the sheets into twelve 8-inch (20 cm) squares. Divide the spinach into 6 portions. At the centre of each square of pasta, arrange a portion in a ring like a doughnut with a 1-inch (2.5 cm) hole. Place an egg yolk inside each spinach ring. Working with 1 ravioli at a time, brush the pasta outside the spinach ring with the egg wash. Place a second sheet of pasta on top, and press the 2 sheets together to seal tightly while carefully pushing as much air from the ravioli as possible. When all 6 ravioli are complete, trim the excess pasta with a knife, in a square or circle as you prefer, leaving at least ½ inch (1 cm) between the spinach and the outside edge.

Cook the ravioli in boiling, salted water for about 2 minutes. Meanwhile, heat a medium saucepan on medium heat, add 1 tbsp (15 mL) cold water, and when it begins to bubble, lower the heat. Add a cube of butter and whisk until it emulsifies. Continue adding butter, a piece at a time, until all the butter is incorporated.

Using a slotted spoon, gently transfer the ravioli to 6 warm serving plates. Pour about 1 tbsp (15 mL) of emulsified butter over each. Season with salt and pepper. Garnish with truffle shavings and a good drizzle of fine olive oil.

Substitutions: There is no true replacement for a fresh truffle, but there are good options for attempting to simulate its flavour. If you cannot find or do not wish to purchase a fresh truffle, consider adding a brunoise of preserved truffle to the butter sauce. Failing that, a good drizzle of white truffle oil goes a long way.

Suggested Wine: Barbaresco

Ravioli di Cervella di Vitello con Puré di Mais
Veal Brain Ravioli with Sweet Corn Purée

Veal brains have a uniquely rich and creamy quality. They are delicious seared all on their own as well as worked into a sauce. Here we cook them twice and then combine them with ricotta to make a robustly satisfying filling for ravioli served in rich veal stock.

Serves 6 as a main course

2 veal brains (about 1 lb/500 g total)
4 tsp (20 mL) white vinegar
½ yellow onion, chopped
Juice of ½ lemon
4 sprigs thyme
2 bay leaves
½ tsp (2 mL) black peppercorns
Salt
3 tbsp (50 mL) olive oil
1 lb (500 g) ricotta (preferably buffalo),
    drained in cheesecloth for 24 hours
1 small yellow onion, lightly caramelized, chilled
1 tbsp (15 mL) minced sage
1 tbsp (15 mL) minced parsley
¾ tsp (3 mL) grated lemon zest
2 pinches of nutmeg
Flour for dusting
1 batch basic pasta dough (page 108)
1 egg, lightly beaten
1 quart (1 L) veal stock (page 286)
2 cobs sweet corn, shucked and poached
2 cups (500 mL) 2% milk

GARNISH
⅓ cup (75 mL) blond soffritto (page 285)
Fine olive oil

Place the brains in a bowl, cover with ice water, add the vinegar, and stir gently. Cover and refrigerate for 3 hours. Drain, cover with fresh cold water, and refrigerate, covered, overnight. Drain again. With a sharp knife, trim away the thin skin and blood vessels.

Transfer brains to a saucepan and cover with cold water. Add the chopped onion, lemon juice, thyme, bay leaves, peppercorns, and a generous pinch of salt. Bring to a boil, then reduce heat and simmer for 12 minutes. Shock in ice water. Split brains in half and remove all visible ventricles. Cover with plastic wrap and chill thoroughly.

Cut the brains into slices about ¼ inch (5 mm) thick. In a nonstick skillet, heat the olive oil on medium-high. Season the slices of brain, sear them for about 15 seconds on each side, then remove to a cutting board. Allow to cool to room temperature, then dice them and transfer to a large bowl. Add the ricotta, caramelized onion, sage, parsley, lemon zest, and a pinch of nutmeg. Mix well, and season with salt and pepper.

Roll the pasta into thin sheets and spread on a flour-dusted work surface. Use a 3-inch (8 cm) pasta or cookie cutter to cut out at least 72 discs. Using a 1-inch (2.5 cm) melon baller, place a scoop of the filling at the centre of half the pasta discs. Brush their edges with egg wash, place a second pasta disc on top of each one, and press the 2 pasta sheets together to seal, carefully expelling as much air from the ravioli as possible. Finally, trim all ravioli with a 2½-inch (6.5 cm) cutter. Dust the ravioli lightly with flour and set aside.

Bring the veal stock to a boil and reduce by three-quarters. Strip the corn from the cobs into another saucepan. Add the cobs and the milk, and simmer, uncovered, for 15 minutes. Discard the cobs. In a blender (or with a hand blender), buzz the corn mixture until smooth. Season with salt, pepper, and a pinch of nutmeg. Keep warm.

To finish, boil the ravioli in salted water until they float, about 3 minutes. Place a generous spoonful of the corn purée at the centre of 6 warm pasta bowls. Arrange 6 ravioli around it. Spoon veal reduction over the ravioli. Garnish with a scattering of soffritto and a drizzle of fine olive oil.

Suggested Wine: Soave or Gavi

Funghi Mushrooms

The lot of the mushroom enthusiast has improved immeasurably over recent decades. As recently as the nineties, the local supermarket typically stocked only button mushrooms, some cremini, and the occasional oyster mushroom or flabby portobello. Now cultivated mushrooms of quality, like the unfailingly flavoursome shiitake and the texturally rewarding king oyster, are mainstays. So too the sweet, delicate enoki. And courtesy of our better markets, Canadians are finally getting to tuck into a previously squandered natural resource: wild lobster mushrooms, blue foot, chanterelles, morels, and matsutake are available everywhere from Granville Island market to the Halifax Farmer's Market.

Alas, the most elusive specimen remains the one that Italians prize most: *Boletus edulis*, the porcini (or *cèpe*, to the French). Domestic sources are scarce, and the more abundant harvest from Oregon seldom materializes here. This leaves us to choose between dried or frozen porcini. Dried ones maintain tremendous flavour, and so when reconstituted, they are ideal for sauces of any kind. The best frozen examples boast surprisingly good texture, and so are best suited to the grill or the sauté pan, and for inclusion in a risotto.

Pappardelle con Costolette e Peperoncino
Pappardelle with Shredded Braised Short Ribs and Chili

This pasta dish is sufficiently pleasing that you may well want to make a tiny batch of braised short ribs exclusively for this purpose—and if so, dividing the short ribs recipe included on page 194 by three will generate enough meat and sauce for the dish described. But this dish is best thought of as a great way to use up leftover short ribs after a dinner party. Serves 6 as an appetizer or 4 as a main course

14 oz (420 g) dry or 20 oz (600 g) fresh pappardelle
2 tbsp (30 mL) olive oil
¼ cup (60 mL) diced onion
1 large clove garlic, minced
2 braised short ribs (page 194), shredded (about 2 cups/500 mL)
¼ cup (60 mL) white wine
2 cups (500 mL) strained short rib braising liquid, reduced until it coats back of a spoon
½ cup (125 mL) basic tomato sauce (page 82)
1 cup (250 mL) torn basil
½ cup (125 mL) minced parsley
1 tbsp (15 mL) minced oil-preserved red chilies
2 tbsp (30 mL) butter
Salt and pepper

GARNISH
Fine olive oil
Grated Pecorino Romano or Parmigiano-Reggiano

Begin cooking the pasta. Meanwhile, in a sauté pan cook the onion in the olive oil until translucent. Add the garlic and cook a minute longer. Add the shredded short ribs, heat through, then deglaze with the wine. Stir in the braising liquid, tomato sauce, basil, parsley, and chilies; heat through. Finally, stir in the butter, and season.

Drain the pasta, reserving 1 cup (250 mL) cooking water. Pour the sauce over the pasta with half of the reserved pasta water. Fold over low heat until pasta and sauce are nicely combined. If it seems dry, add more pasta water. Taste, and correct seasonings. Serve drizzled with olive oil and topped with grated pecorino.

Substitution: You can of course deglaze with red wine instead of white. White wine simply yields a lighter result—which provides a welcome balance in this dish.

Suggested Wine: Tuscan IGT

Bucatini all'Amatriciana
Bucatini with Guanciale and Spicy Tomato Sauce

This Roman classic from the town of Amatrice is a great dish to have in your culinary arsenal, for it is as quick and easy to prepare as it is rewarding to consume. The guanciale adds a lot of flavour to the mix. If this is not readily available, you can make a satisfying version of the dish with pancetta. **Serves 6 as an appetizer or 4 as a main course**

14 oz (420 g) dry or 20 oz (600 g) fresh bucatini
2 tbsp (30 mL) olive oil
4 oz (125 g) guanciale, julienned
¼ cup (60 mL) diced onion
1 large clove garlic, minced
¼ cup (60 mL) white wine
2 tbsp (30 mL) chopped oil-preserved red chilies (preferably Calabrese)
2 cups (500 mL) basic tomato sauce (page 82)
Salt and pepper
2 tbsp (30 mL) chopped parsley
2 tbsp (30 mL) butter

Begin cooking the pasta. Meanwhile, in a large skillet, heat the oil on medium-high. Add the guanciale and sauté until it begins to crisp at the edges, about 2 minutes. Lower heat to medium, add the onion, and cook, stirring, until it wilts—but do not let it acquire any colour. Add the garlic, cook 1 minute longer, then deglaze with the wine. Stir in the chilies. When the wine has reduced to a syrup, add the tomato sauce. Season—but salt lightly, in deference to the salty guanciale. Stir in the parsley and butter, taste, and correct seasonings.

Drain the pasta, reserving 1 cup (250 mL) cooking water. Pour the sauce over the pasta with half of the reserved pasta water. Fold over low heat until the pasta and sauce are nicely combined. If it seems dry, add more pasta water. Taste, and correct seasonings.

Suggested Wine: Chianti Classico

Gnocchi di Ricotta con Salsa al Pomodoro
Ricotta Gnocchi with Heirloom Tomato Sauce

In their customary potato-based makeup, gnocchi amount to a dish of heft and substance. These ones however are made of ricotta, bound with only a modicum of flour—and so they are feather-light. Paired with this lightly cooked tomato sauce, they make a perfect summer dish.

Serves 6 as an appetizer or 4 as a main course

2 lb (1 kg) ricotta (preferably buffalo)
1 egg, plus 1 egg yolk
⅔ cup (150 mL) all-purpose flour, plus additional
    for dusting
½ tbsp (7 mL) kosher salt
¼ tsp (1 mL) black pepper

Grated zest of ½ lemon
1 batch heirloom tomato sauce (page 82)
2 tbsp (30 mL) butter, preferably whipped
1 top-quality burrata (about 8 oz/250 g)
2 tbsp (30 mL) fine olive oil
12 basil leaves, torn

Rinse a sheet of cheesecloth under cold running water, squeeze it dry, and line a large strainer with it. Place the strainer over a bowl, add the ricotta, cover, and refrigerate overnight. The next day, discard the drained liquid, wipe the bowl dry, and tip in the thickened ricotta. Press down on the centre of the mound to form a well. Add the egg and egg yolk, and gently mix into the ricotta with your hands, lifting the mixture and then letting it tumble between your fingers so that it is aerated by the process. Sift the flour over the mixture, then add the salt, pepper, and lemon zest; gently mix together as before. The dough should be just tacky to the touch—if it feels wet and sticky, incorporate a little more flour.

Flour a work surface and then, working in batches of about a handful at a time, roll the dough into a log about ¾ inch (2.5 cm) wide. Flour a knife and trim the end of the log at an angle. Maintaining that angle, cut the roll into equal pieces about 1 inch (2.5 cm) long. Transfer the gnocchi to a lightly floured baking sheet.

Bring a large pot of salted water to a vigorous boil. Add the gnocchi, and stir very gently to prevent them from sticking. As they float to the surface—after about 2 minutes—remove them with a slotted spoon to a lightly oiled baking sheet to cool.

In a large skillet or sauté pan on medium-high heat, bring the tomato sauce to a simmer. Add the cooled gnocchi and stir very gently to cover them with the sauce. When the gnocchi are heated through, taste and correct seasonings. Gently stir in the butter. Divide gnocchi and sauce among warm plates or pasta bowls. Working over a plate, tear the burrata into bite-sized pieces and then divide them—along with the leaked cream—among the servings. Garnish each plate with a drizzle of olive oil and a scattering of basil.

Substitutions: Clumps of fresh burrata melting on contact with hot tomato sauce makes for a special experience, but if you are unable to locate one of unimpeachable freshness, 1 cup (250 mL) freshly grated Parmigiano-Reggiano or Pecorino Romano makes an eminently suitable substitute.

Suggested Wine: Chianti

Gnocchi con Ragù d'Agnello e Ricotta alla Menta
Gnocchi with Lamb Bolognese and Mint Ricotta

Ragù in the Bolognese style often features ground meat, as opposed to larger cuts braised in cubes or chunks and then shredded. This recipe features lamb rather than beef, and is a lot richer for it. Note, too, that it is easy and quick to prepare.

Serves 8 as an appetizer or 6 as a main course

2 tbsp (30 mL) olive oil
½ medium Spanish onion, minced
1 large clove garlic, minced
2 lb (1 kg) ground lamb
1 tbsp (15 mL) chopped oregano
1 tbsp (15 mL) chopped mint
1 tbsp (15 mL) chopped basil
1 tsp (5 mL) toasted fennel seeds, crushed
1 cup (250 mL) white wine
1½ cans (each 28 oz/796 mL) San Marzano tomatoes
¼ cup (60 mL) tomato paste
Salt and pepper
1 batch potato gnocchi (page 282)

GARNISH
½ cup ricotta di bufala, drained in cheesecloth
for 24 hours
Juice of ½ lemon
3 tbsp (50 mL) chopped mint
2 tbsp (30 mL) 35% cream
1 tbsp (15 mL) olive oil
Salt and pepper
Fine olive oil

In a Dutch oven, sweat the onion in the olive oil. When it begins to wilt, add the garlic and sweat a minute longer. Raise heat to medium-high and add the lamb, breaking it up with a wooden spoon and stirring vigorously to prevent the meat from sticking. After about 10 minutes, when the meat is largely browned, with only traces of pink, stir in the oregano, mint, basil, and fennel seeds. Follow immediately with the wine. When that has nearly evaporated, add the tomatoes and tomato paste, crushing the tomatoes with the side of your spoon as you stir. Bring to a simmer, season lightly, and then reduce heat to its lowest possible setting. Simmer, uncovered and stirring periodically, for 40 minutes. Taste, adjust seasonings, and maintain at a bare simmer.

Begin cooking the gnocchi. Meanwhile, prepare the garnish by combining the ricotta, lemon juice, mint, cream, and olive oil in a bowl and mixing well. Season to taste. Drain the gnocchi, return to the pot, add the desired amount of sauce, and toss. Taste, and adjust seasonings. Divide gnocchi among warm serving bowls, and top each portion with a dollop of mint ricotta and a drizzle of fine olive oil.

Suggested Wine: Bolgheri Cabernet Franc or Brunello

Gnocchi al Guanciale di Vitello
Gnocchi with Shredded Veal Cheek

As a cow likes nothing more than to chew its cud, its cheeks are the fittest muscles on its body. That translates into great flavour. This cut is also layered with fat and connective tissue, and so responds beautifully when slowly braised, yielding an irresistibly rich sauce. Add gnocchi, and all is good. **Serves 6 as an appetizer or 4 as a main course**

1½ lb (750 g) veal cheeks, trimmed of all silverskin
½ medium Spanish onion, chopped
2 stalks celery, chopped
1 medium carrot, chopped
3 cloves garlic, chopped
4 sprigs sage
3 sprigs rosemary
3 bay leaves
2 cups (500 mL) Barolo
⅓ cup (75 mL) olive oil

Salt and pepper
1 can (12 oz/341 mL) San Marzano tomatoes
3 cups (750 mL) veal stock (page 286)
1 batch potato gnocchi (page 282)
2 tbsp (30 mL) butter

GARNISH
½ cup (125 mL) grated Pecorino Romano
   or Parmigiano-Reggiano
Fine olive oil

In a bowl or snug sealable container, combine veal cheeks, onion, celery, carrot, garlic, sage, rosemary, and bay leaves. Pour over the Barolo, and if necessary, jiggle the contents to ensure they are submerged in the wine. Cover and refrigerate overnight.

Preheat oven to 300°F (150°C).

Remove veal cheeks from the marinade and shake off excess; reserve the marinade. Pat veal dry with paper towels, massage with a little of the olive oil, and season generously. In a Dutch oven on medium-high, heat 3 tbsp (50 mL) of the oil. Sear the veal until nicely browned on all sides. Remove the veal to a plate. Pour out the oil and wipe the pot with a paper towel. Return the pot to the heat and add the remaining olive oil. Strain the marinade, reserving both liquid and solids. Add the wine-soaked vegetables and herbs to the pot and sauté until caramelized. Add the tomatoes and reduce slightly, about 5 minutes. Return the veal to the pot along with the juices from its plate. Add the marinade; reduce by half. Add the veal stock and bring to a simmer. Cover the pot, transfer to the oven, and braise for 2½ hours. Test the cheeks for tenderness—the meat should be easy to pull apart. If not, return the pot to the oven, testing every 15 minutes until the meat is tender.

Let the braise cool slightly. Discard the herb sprigs and bay leaves. Remove the veal cheeks to a platter. Briefly blitz the sauce with in a blender (or with a hand blender) to break up large chunks—but not so much as to render it completely smooth. Return the sauce to the pot. Use a pair of forks to shred the meat, and reintroduce it to the sauce. Reheat the ragù, taste, and adjust the seasonings.

Meanwhile, cook the gnocchi until they float, about 3 minutes. Using a slotted spoon, transfer the gnocchi to the sauce. Toss, and correct seasonings. Stir in the butter. Divide among warm bowls, and garnish with cheese and a drizzle of olive oil.

Suggested Wine: Valpolicella

Risotto

Basic Risotto

The procedure for preparing risotto outlined below serves as a basis for all our risotto recipes—which always begin the same way, even if the flavour is built with a different broth or stock. They are invariably finished the same way too, after the addition of their respective principal ingredients. Always remember the simple rule that the more you stir the rice, the more starch will be extracted from it, resulting in a creamier mix. With experience you'll discover just how much stirring suits your particular taste.

Serves 6 as an appetizer or 4 as a main course

3 tbsp (50 mL) olive oil
1 cup (250 mL) minced onion
Salt
1 tsp (5 mL) minced garlic
1½ cups (325 mL) carnaroli rice
½ cup (125 mL) white wine
5 cups (1.25 L) white *brodo* (page 3), at a simmer
¼ cup (60 mL) freshly grated Parmigiano-Reggiano
2 tbsp (30 mL) butter
2 tbsp (30 mL) truffle paste (optional)
Ground white pepper

Heat 2 tbsp (30 mL) of the oil in a heavy pot over medium heat. Add the onions, salt lightly, and sweat, stirring frequently so that the onions do not brown. When after 5 or 6 minutes the onions begin to wilt, add the garlic and cook a minute longer. Add the rice and stir well to coat with the oil. Add more oil if necessary. Continue cooking, stirring frequently, until the grains of rice begin to acquire translucence (if uncertain, lift a few grains from the pot and examine them against the dark backdrop of your wooden spoon). When that is achieved, deglaze with the wine.

When the wine has been reduced to a syrup add ½ cup (125 mL) of the hot *brodo*. Stir again. When the liquid once again thickens, add another ¼ cup (60 mL) *brodo* and stir again. Season lightly. Stir regularly, and build the seasoning gradually as you go. Continue until the rice is nearly cooked and the stock nearly finished.

Stir the primary seasoning into the risotto. Add the cheese, and stir until heated through. Remove from the heat and stir in the butter and optional truffle paste. Taste, and correct seasonings with salt and white pepper. Serve with the appropriate garnish.

Substitutions: We only use carnaroli rice for risotto at Fabbrica and the other McEwan restaurants. Vialone nano is in our opinion a close second and arborio a distant third. You may use chicken stock (page 286) in place of the white *brodo*. Our regular *brodo* is a dark stock, and so it will yield an inappropriately dark risotto. If you must use it, dilute it with water by at least a third.

Risotto con Midollo Arrosto
Risotto with Roast Marrow and Veal *Jus*

Roast bone marrow is as indulgently rich as foie gras at a fraction of the cost. Here, we fold crisp discs of marrow into creamy risotto to magnificent effect. It works as well for a starter as it does as a side dish to any grilled or roasted meat. **Serves 6 as an appetizer**

4 beef marrow bones (each about 6 inches/18 cm
    and 4 lb/2 kg total), split lengthwise
Flour for dusting
Salt and pepper
3 tbsp (50 mL) clarified butter
1 batch basic risotto (page 146)
¼ cup (60 mL) freshly grated Parmigiano-Reggiano
2 tbsp (30 mL) butter
2 tbsp (30 mL) truffle paste (optional)
Ground white pepper

GARNISH
¼ cup (60 mL) veal *jus*
2 tbsp (30 mL) minced chives
Truffle shavings (optional)

Soak the marrow bones as described on page 275. Roast half of them according to the same recipe. After they have cooled, remove the marrow, chop roughly, and set aside. Meanwhile, pat the remaining bones dry, and using the handle of a spoon (not your fingers, for fear of bone shards), force the raw marrow from the bone—if possible in a single piece. Slice the raw marrow into discs about ¼ inch (5 mm) thick. Dredge the marrow discs in flour, season them generously, and then fry them in the clarified butter over medium-high heat until thoroughly bronzed. Set aside.

Begin cooking the risotto according to the directions on page 146. When the rice is very nearly cooked, stir in the roasted marrow. Add the cheese, and stir until heated through. Remove from the heat and stir in the butter and optional truffle paste. Taste, and correct seasonings with salt and white pepper. Serve studded with the discs of pan-fried bone marrow. Garnish with a drizzle of veal *jus*, chives, and optional truffle shavings.

Substitutions: If you want to provide this deliciously rich recipe with a further flavour that we employ in the restaurant, use bone marrow butter (page 275) in place of the regular butter.

Suggested Wine: Barolo or Barbaresco

Risotto ai Funghi e Tartufo
Risotto with Mushrooms and Shaved Truffle

There is not much in the Italian idiom of flavour—or anybody's—that goes together as well as mushroom, truffle, and Parmigiano-Reggiano. When incorporated in a risotto, the combination is unfailingly sublime. **Serves 6 as an appetizer or side dish**

3 cups (750 mL) mixed top-quality mushrooms
    (porcini, chanterelles, blue foot, etc.)
1 tbsp (15 mL) olive oil
¼ tsp (1 mL) minced rosemary
Squeeze of lemon juice
Salt and pepper
1 batch basic risotto (page 146)
¼ cup (60 mL) truffle paste
¼ cup (60 mL) freshly grated Parmigiano-Reggiano
2 tbsp (30 mL) butter
Ground white pepper

GARNISH
3 tbsp (50 mL) freshly grated Parmigiano-Reggiano
1 small truffle (about 3 oz/90 g)
Truffle oil

Clean the mushrooms. Trim off the stems, add them to the vegetable stock to be used to prepare the risotto, and simmer for 1 hour. Strain the stock and discard the stems. (This step may be omitted, in which case simply discard the stems.) Slice the mushrooms about ¼ inch (5 mm) thick. In a sauté pan on medium heat, cook the mushrooms in the olive oil until they wilt. When their liquid evaporates, stir in the rosemary, deglaze the pan with lemon juice, season, and set aside.

Begin cooking the risotto according to the directions on page 146, using vegetable stock in place of the *brodo*. When the rice is about 5 minutes away from being done, stir in the mushrooms. When the rice is very close to cooked, and the supply of stock virtually exhausted, stir in the truffle paste. Add the cheese, and stir until heated through. Remove from the heat and stir in the butter. Taste, and correct seasonings with salt and white pepper. Serve sprinkled with Parmesan, scattered with truffle shavings, and drizzled with truffle oil.

Substitutions: If you have no vegetable stock, chicken stock (page 286) should be your second choice and white *brodo* (page 3), your third. As with the vegetable stock, these will also benefit from an infusion of simmered mushroom trimmings for this particular recipe.

Suggested Wine: Barolo

Risotto ai Frutti di Mare
Risotto with Mixed Seafood

The mix of seafood included in this classic Italian dish should always reflect what is fresh and in prime season at your local fishmonger rather than what is listed in the recipe. Needless to say, lobster works beautifully in place of the shrimp, a small fillet of firm monkfish can supplant the scallops, and so on. **Serves 4 as a main course**

1 batch basic risotto (page 146)
1 tbsp (15 mL) olive oil
½ yellow onion, sliced
1 clove garlic, smashed
2 sprigs thyme
16 clams, scrubbed and flushed (see page 7)
24 mussels, scrubbed and debearded
½ cup (125 mL) white wine
8 medium shrimp, shelled, deveined, and split lengthwise
4 large scallops, halved crosswise, then quartered
   (8 pieces each)

4 oz (125 g) cooked crabmeat, picked over and
   broken into chunks
½ cup (75 mL) basic tomato sauce (page 82)
12 basil leaves
1 tbsp (15 mL) chopped parsley
2 tbsp (30 mL) freshly grated Parmigiano-Reggiano
2 tbsp (30 mL) butter
Ground white pepper
Squeeze of lemon juice

Begin cooking the risotto according to the directions on page 146, but use fish stock or vegetable stock in place of the white *brodo*.

Meanwhile, in a sauté pan over medium heat, cook the onion and garlic in the olive oil until they begin to soften. Add the thyme and cook a minute longer. Raise the heat and add the clams, mussels, and white wine. Bring to a boil, lower the heat, and cover the pan. After about 2 minutes, begin removing the mussels as they pop open. Cover again, and a few minutes later do the same with the clams. (Discard any that do not open.) Strain the cooking liquid and add it to the simmering fish stock you are using to cook the risotto.

When the risotto is a few minutes away from being cooked, add a double ladle of fish stock to the pot, and when it begins to bubble, stir in the shrimp. One minute later follow with the scallops, and 1 minute after that, stir in the crab. Remove about 16 of the mussels from their shells, as well as half the clams, and discard the empty shells. Add the shelled molluscs to the risotto, then stir in the tomato sauce, basil, and parsley. Add the cheese, and stir until heated through. Remove from the heat and stir in the butter. Taste, and correct seasonings with salt and white pepper. Stir in a little lemon juice to finish. Serve on a platter—or divide among 4 warm shallow bowls, with one pair of unshelled clams and mussels in each portion.

Suggested Wine: Trebbiano d'Abruzzo

Risotto con Zucca e Pancetta
Risotto with Sugar Pumpkin and Pancetta

The sweet, rich, creamy nature of sugar pumpkin lends itself perfectly to being showcased in risotto. And pancetta provides exactly the right salty accent. This combination works especially well as a side dish for meat or fish. **Serves 6 as an appetizer or side dish**

1½ cups (375 mL) large-diced sugar pumpkin
1½ cups (375 mL) *brodo* (page 3)
3 tbsp (50 mL) cold butter
Salt and pepper
Pinch of nutmeg
3 tbsp (50 mL) olive oil
¼ cup (60 mL) diced pancetta
1 batch basic risotto (page 146)
¼ cup (60 mL) freshly grated Parmigiano-Reggiano
2 tbsp (30 mL) butter
2 tbsp (30 mL) truffle paste (optional)
Ground white pepper
Fine olive oil

Place 1 cup (250 mL) of the diced pumpkin in a small saucepan, add enough *brodo* to cover, and simmer until mushy, about 30 minutes. Mash the pumpkin with a fork, and then stir vigorously until it becomes a smooth paste. Incorporate the cold butter, then season with salt, pepper, and nutmeg. Set aside.

In a skillet on medium heat, sauté the pancetta in the oil just until it begins to brown and crisp at the edges, then remove it with a slotted spoon to a bed of paper towels to drain. Add the remaining squash to the skillet and sauté until bronzed. Season with salt and pepper and remove to a platter.

Begin cooking the risotto according to the directions on page 146. When the rice is very nearly cooked, and the supply of stock virtually exhausted, add the pancetta, sautéed pumpkin, and ¼ cup (60 mL) of the pumpkin purée. Add the cheese, and stir until heated through. Remove from the heat and stir in the butter and optional truffle paste. Taste, and correct seasonings with salt and white pepper. Serve lightly drizzled with fine olive oil.

Substitutions: Any sweet, firm squash, such as butternut, will serve as a good substitute for the pumpkin.

Suggested Wine: Barbera d'Asti or Cannonau di Sardegna

Risotto all'Anatra e Olive Nere
Risotto with Braised Duck and Black Olives

This dish was conceived to be served with goose, but outside of Europe, the butcher shop that sells single goose legs is regrettably hard to come by. Two duck legs do the same work here as one from a goose, but if you do come into a plump leg from the larger bird, do give it a try. Both birds have rich, dark leg meat, and the olives are the perfect salty counterpoint to either. **Serves 6 as an appetizer or 4 as a main course**

2 tbsp (30 mL) olive oil
2 duck legs (each about 8 oz/250 g)
Salt and pepper
½ medium carrot, diced
½ stalk celery, diced
½ Spanish onion, diced
1 clove garlic, crushed
1 sprig rosemary
1 sprig thyme
1 sprig sage, plus 4 leaves, chopped
¾ cup (175 mL) Barolo

2 cups (500 mL) *brodo* (page 3)
1 batch basic risotto (page 146)
¾ cup (175 mL) infornate olives, pitted and halved
¼ cup (60 mL) freshly grated Parmigiano-Reggiano
2 tbsp (30 mL) butter
2 tbsp (30 mL) truffle paste (optional)
Ground white pepper

GARNISH
Minced chives
Chopped crispy duck skin (optional)

Preheat oven to 300°F (150°C).

Rub the duck legs with a little of the olive oil and season them generously. Heat the remaining oil in a sauté pan on medium-high. Sear the duck until bronzed on both sides; remove from the pan and set aside. Add the carrot, celery, onion, garlic, rosemary, thyme, and sage sprig to the pan; sauté until wilted and lightly coloured. Deglaze with ¼ cup (60 mL) of the wine. When that has evaporated, return the duck legs to the pan with the rest of the wine. When the wine has reduced by half, add the *brodo*. Bring to a boil, then cover, transfer to the oven, and braise until the duck is tender and yields easily when pierced with a fork, about 1¼ hours.

Remove the duck legs from their braising liquid and set aside. Strain the liquid into a saucepan, skim off the fat, and reduce by about half—until it thickens enough to coat the back of a spoon. Season, and set aside on low heat. Strip the duck meat from its bones, tear into bite-sized morsels; cover and set aside.

Begin cooking the risotto according to the directions on page 146. When the rice is very nearly cooked, and the supply of stock virtually exhausted, add the shredded duck and olives. When that is heated through, add the cheese, and again stir until heated through. Remove from the heat and stir in the butter and optional truffle paste. Taste, and correct seasonings with salt and white pepper. Drizzle with the Barolo reduction, and garnish with chives and the optional duck skin.

Substitutions: You can use chicken stock in place of the *brodo*. The distinctive quality of the Barolo helps create a better reduction for the risotto, so do not use a different red wine.

Suggested Wine: Pinot Nero or Barbaresco

Risotto al Salmone e Asparagi
Risotto with Flaked Salmon and Asparagus

Salmon is most assuredly not native to Italy, but all the same, the nation that carries the flag for slow, local food began a culinary love affair with the fish sometime in the 1980s that has never abated. While risotto is heavy by nature, think of this particular mix as an ideal one for spring or summer. Always serve it as a course unto itself and never as a side dish—it does not work alongside anything. **Serves 6 as an appetizer or 4 as a main course**

1 large fillet Atlantic salmon (about 12 oz/375 g)
3 tbsp (50 mL) olive oil
Salt and pepper
¼ cup (60 mL) julienned guanciale
1 batch basic risotto (page 146)
12 spears asparagus, blanched and cut into 1½-inch (4 cm) pieces
2 tbsp (30 mL) freshly grated Parmigiano-Reggiano
2 tbsp (30 mL) butter
Ground white pepper
Squeeze of lemon juice

GARNISH
1 tbsp (15 mL) minced chives
Raw asparagus shavings (optional)
Chopped crispy salmon skin (optional)
Fine olive oil

Preheat oven to 375° (190°C).

Rub the salmon with a little of the olive oil and season it generously on both sides. In a nonstick skillet, sauté the guanciale in 2 tbsp (30 mL) of the oil until it crisps at the edges, about 2 minutes. Remove with a slotted spoon and drain on paper towels. Add the salmon to the pan skin side up. When the salmon has bronzed, flip it over and crisp the skin, about 4 minutes more. Transfer the pan to the oven until the fish is cooked medium-rare, about 6 minutes. Set aside to cool to room temperature.

Begin preparing the risotto as described on page 146, using vegetable stock or fish stock in place of the brodo. When the rice is very nearly cooked, and the supply of stock virtually exhausted, peel the skin from the salmon and then crumble and flake the fish directly into the risotto. (If desired, reserve the crispy skin to chop for garnish.) Stir, and then follow with the asparagus. When that is heated through, add the cheese, and again stir until heated through. Remove from the heat and stir in the butter. Taste, and correct seasonings with salt and white pepper. Finish with the lemon juice. Serve garnished with chives, optional asparagus shavings, optional crispy salmon skin, and a drizzle of fine olive oil.

Substitutions: You may use about 1 cup (250 mL) of blanched sweet spring peas in place of the asparagus. The fish component needs to be both flaky and firm, with good oil content, so stick to related species, like Tasmanian ocean trout or a local steelhead.

Suggested Wine: Ribolla Gialla or Vernaccia

Pesce
Fish

Orata alla Griglia con Capperi e Menta
Grilled Sea Bream with Capers and Mint

The flaky flesh of the sea bream has a high oil content that makes it almost uniquely suited to the grill. Cooked properly there, its skin will be rendered deliciously crispy, and its flesh moist and mildly smoky from the dripping fat burning on the coals below. These qualities combine beautifully with this rustic stuffing of mint, parsley, and capers. **Serves 4**

4 whole sea bream (each about 1 lb/500 g), cleaned, scaled, and heads removed
Salt and pepper
1 tbsp (15 mL) combined minced oregano, thyme, rosemary, sage, and parsley
¾ cup (175 mL) olive oil
4 cloves garlic, thinly sliced

¼ loaf focaccia
3 tbsp (50 mL) salt-packed capers, soaked, rinsed, and drained
⅓ cup (75 mL) torn mint leaves
⅓ cup (75 mL) roughly chopped parsley
1 tbsp (15 mL) chopped chives
1 lemon, cut into eighths

Fillet (or ask your fishmonger to fillet) the sea bream in such a way that they remain attached at the tail, as if it were a hinge. Make 3 parallel slashes about ¼ inch (5 mm) deep in the skin side of each fillet (6 per fish). Rub a generous pinch of salt into each incision. Open the fish and season the inside with salt and pepper. Mix the minced herbs with 4 tsp (20 mL) of the olive oil and massage the inside of each fish with it. Reassemble the fish and set aside in the refrigerator.

In a skillet over low heat, gently sweat the garlic in ½ cup (125 mL) of the olive oil until it wilts. Meanwhile, with your fingers, pull crouton-sized morsels of focaccia from between the crusts until you have about ½ cup (125 mL). Remove the garlic from the oil with a slotted spoon and discard it. Raise heat to medium-low, add the focaccia, and cook until the croutons are crisp on all sides, about 5 minutes. With a slotted spoon, remove the croutons to a plate, salt lightly, and set aside. Allow oil to cool to room temperature.

Preheat grill on medium. Oil the grill with the remaining olive oil, and then place the fish on the grill at an angle, rotating them after 2 or 3 minutes to cross-hatch them. After another 2 or 3 minutes, carefully flip them over. Cook the second side, without rotating, about 4 minutes. Arrange the fish cross-hatched side up on 4 warm plates to rest. Meanwhile, in a bowl, combine reserved garlic-crouton oil with the capers, mint, parsley, and chives; toss well. Spoon the mixture over the fish. Top each fish with a few croutons and 2 wedges of lemon.

Substitutions: As always, you may use less-flavoursome brined capers in place of salt-packed ones if need be. This presentation of grilled bream works nicely with any whole white fish that has high oil content and grills well—such as branzino.

Side Dish Suggestions: Sautéed Swiss Chard with White Anchovies and Lemon Zest; Roman Cauliflower with Cheese Sauce; Braised Fennel with Tomato and Sambuca

Suggested Wine: Vernaccia or Trebbiano

Trota con Vongole e Salsiccia
Rainbow Trout with Clams and Italian Sausage

When you pan-roast a fresh fillet of trout to give it crisp skin along with its firm, sweet flesh, it needs little other enhancement. But whether it needs it or not, it still tastes better with a side of salty steamed clams. Here we add a little spicy sausage meat to the mix, and bind it all with butter, lemon, and a hint of tomato. **Serves 4**

4 tbsp (60 mL) olive oil
1 hot Italian sausage, casing removed
¼ cup (60 mL) minced onion
1 clove garlic, minced
2 lb (1 kg) clams, scrubbed and flushed (see page 7)
½ cup (125 mL) white wine
4 trout fillets (each about 8 oz/250 g)
Salt and pepper
1 tbsp (15 mL) basic tomato sauce (page 82)
1 tbsp (15 mL) butter
1 tbsp (15 mL) minced parsley
Squeeze of lemon juice
1 tbsp (15 mL) fine olive oil

Set a rack in the top shelf of the oven and preheat oven to 375°F (190°C).

Heat 1 tbsp (15 mL) of the olive oil in a small skillet on medium heat. Add the sausage meat, break it up with a wooden spoon, and stir until it is lightly browned, about 5 minutes. Remove from the heat and set aside.

In a large skillet or sauté pan, sweat the onion in 2 tbsp (30 mL) of the olive oil until it begins to wilt, about 3 minutes. Add the garlic and sweat a minute longer. Add the clams, raise the heat, and add the white wine. Let boil for 1 minute, then cover and lower heat to a simmer.

In a large nonstick skillet over medium-high, heat the remaining 1 tbsp (15 mL) olive oil. Pat trout fillets dry and season on both sides with salt and pepper. Add the fillets, skin side down, to the pan. When, after 2 or 3 minutes, the skin begins to crisp, transfer the skillet to the oven until the fish is cooked through, about 4 minutes.

Arrange the fish on 4 warm plates (or a platter) skin side up. As the clams begin popping open, arrange them around the fillets. (Discard any that do not open.) Raise heat and reduce cooking liquid by half. Stir in the tomato sauce and sausage meat. When heated through, stir in the butter, parsley, and lemon juice. Adjust the seasonings and spoon over the fish and clams. Drizzle with olive oil and serve.

Substitutions: At Fabbrica we sometimes make this dish with rainbow trout and sometimes with steelhead trout farmed in B.C. Any quality trout will do. You can also make the dish with a whole fish, as pictured, and fillet it at the table.

Suggested Wine: Greco di Tufo

Ippoglosso con Pomodori Ciliegini e Crostini al Midollo
Roast Halibut with Cherry Tomatoes and Bone Marrow Croutons

When halibut is in season, its flesh firm and mildly sweet, it marries perfectly with this play on panzanella—a combination of charred and cured cherry tomatoes with bone marrow croutons, invigorated with reduced wine and red wine vinegar. **Serves 6**

1 large skinless fillet halibut (about 2 lb/1 kg)
Salt and white pepper
¼ cup (60 mL) olive oil
2 tbsp (30 mL) butter
1½ cups (375 mL) yellow cherry tomatoes
½ cup (125 mL) olive-oil-packed red cherry tomatoes
1 cup (250 mL) bone marrow focaccia croutons (page 276)
¼ cup (60 mL) white wine
1 tbsp (15 mL) red wine vinegar
2 beef marrow bones (each about 6 inches/18 cm), marrow only,
    split, soaked, and fried (optional; see page 147)
2 tbsp (30 mL) chopped basil
1 tbsp (15 mL) chopped parsley
Salt and pepper
2 tbsp (30 mL) fine olive oil

Preheat oven to 375°F (190°C).

Pat the halibut dry with paper towels and season with salt and white pepper. Heat half the olive oil in a large nonstick skillet on medium-high. Add the fish skin side up and sear until lightly bronzed, about 5 minutes. Add half of the butter, flip the fish, and transfer to the oven. Roast the fish, basting periodically, until it is cooked through and beginning to flake, about 10 minutes, depending on the thickness of the fillet.

Meanwhile, heat another skillet on high heat, add the remaining olive oil and butter, and sear the yellow tomatoes until they blister, split, and begin to break down. Add the red tomatoes and then the croutons. Deglaze the pan with the white wine, and then follow with the vinegar. Working quickly—you want the croutons to be moistened but not soggy—fold in the optional fried bone marrow, basil, and parsley. Season.

Transfer the fish to a warm platter, top with the tomato-crouton mixture, and drizzle with the olive oil. Cut into portions at the table and serve topped with the hot panzanella and its juices.

Side Dish Suggestions: Risotto with Sugar Pumpkin and Pancetta; Sautéed Swiss Chard with White Anchovies and Lemon Zest (anchovy optional)

Suggested Wine: Pinot Nero or Nerello Mascalese

Tonno alla Puttanesca
Tuna with Puttanesca Sauce

In the West, until a quarter-century ago when Japanese cuisine went mainstream, tuna was traditionally cooked until medium—at least—at the centre. Searing it lightly yields a more pleasing texture but a lot less flavour. Marking the fish on the grill and then poaching it in olive oil is the ultimate compromise—and combining it with this robust classic of pasta sauces enhances the flavour immeasurably. **Serves 4**

1 quart (1 L) olive oil
½ yellow onion, diced
1 tsp (5 mL) minced garlic
1 cup (250 mL) Cerignola olives, pitted and chopped
1 tbsp (15 mL) capers, rinsed and drained
3 oil-preserved red chilies, minced
8 anchovy fillets (preferably salt-packed),
    rinsed and drained
½ cup (125 mL) white wine
1 can (14 oz/398 mL) San Marzano tomatoes, crushed

1 tbsp (15 mL) minced oregano
1 tbsp (15 mL) minced parsley
Leaves from 4 sprigs basil, plus 16 leaves for garnish
Salt and pepper
4 skinless fillets albacore tuna (each about 5 oz/150 g)
A few drops of hot pepper sauce, red wine vinegar,
    or lemon juice
1 tbsp (15 mL) cold butter, preferably whipped
Fine olive oil

In a sauté pan on medium-low heat, sweat the onion in 1 tbsp (15 mL) of the olive oil until it wilts. Add the garlic and cook another minute. Stir in the olives, capers, chilies, and anchovies. Raise the heat to medium-high and deglaze with the wine. When that has nearly evaporated, add the tomatoes. When the sauce begins to bubble, lower the heat. Add the oregano, parsley, and basil, season lightly, and stir well. Simmer, uncovered, until the sauce thickens, about 30 minutes.

Meanwhile, preheat grill (or a grill pan) on high. Rub the tuna fillets with a little of the olive oil and season them. In a saucepan large enough to accommodate the tuna fillets without their sides touching, heat the remaining olive oil over medium-low heat to a temperature of 140°F (60°C). Lightly cross-hatch both sides of the fillets on the grill; add them to the hot oil. Cook until the fish begins to firm up but remains rare at the centre, about 8 minutes. Remove the fish from the oil with a slotted spoon and season on both sides.

Taste the sauce and adjust its acidity with a few drops of hot sauce, vinegar, or lemon juice. Adjust the seasonings. Stir in the butter until melted. Pool a quarter of the sauce in the centre of each of 4 warm serving plates. Slice each tuna fillet into 5 equal pieces and arrange the slices like tumbled domino tiles over the sauce. Scatter basil leaves around the fish and finish with a generous drizzle of fine olive oil.

Variation: Poaching in olive oil gives flavoursome results because its gentle heat yields fish with a range of incrementally—rather than abruptly—evolving doneness. But you may prefer to save time and effort and simply sear the fish. To do that, pat the fish dry, rub it with a little olive oil, season thoroughly, and cook on a hot oiled grill (or in a skillet with 2 tbsp/30 mL olive oil) to desired doneness.

Substitutions: Grilled swordfish also works very well with the puttanesca sauce. Feel free to use any quality brined olive of your choice in place of the Cerignolas.

Suggested Wine: Sicilian white

Capesante con Pomodori Arrosti, Speck e Acciughe
Seared Scallops with Cured Tomato, Speck, and Anchovy

The finest, freshest scallops have an assertive sweetness to them that finds a compelling counterpoint in this bracingly flavoured sauce. It combines the richness of cured tomato, the saltiness of anchovy, the bite of mustard, and the acidity of vinegar. **Serves 4**

3 oz (90 g) Italian speck, diced
3 oz (90 g) double-smoked bacon, diced
¼ cup (60 mL) grapeseed oil
5 shallots, very thinly sliced
10 anchovy fillets (preferably salt-packed), rinsed, drained, and chopped
¼ cup (60 mL) oven-dried tomatoes, chopped
2 tbsp (30 mL) red wine vinegar
1 tbsp (15 mL) grainy mustard

Salt and pepper
2 tbsp (30 mL) olive oil
12 large sea scallops
3 tbsp (50 mL) butter

GARNISH
1 tbsp (15 mL) chopped parsley
1 tbsp (15 mL) crispy-fried capers (optional; page 278)

Sweat the speck and bacon in half the grapeseed oil until it begins to crisp. Remove the speck and bacon to a bowl with a slotted spoon. Add the shallots to the pan and sweat until wilted. Transfer the shallots and cooking oil to the bowl. Add the anchovies, tomatoes, remaining grapeseed oil, red wine vinegar, and mustard; stir well. Season lightly, cover, and set aside on the counter overnight.

Heat a large nonstick skillet on medium-high. (Use 2 skillets if necessary to avoid crowding and thus steaming the scallops.) Add the olive oil. Pat the scallops dry and season them with salt and pepper. Sear until well bronzed on one side, about 3 minutes. Add the butter, turn the scallops, and cook for another 5 or 6 minutes for medium (or to desired doneness). Remove the scallops from the pan and let rest on 4 warm plates. Pour the fat from the skillet, wipe with a paper towel, and add the speck and anchovy sauce. Stir until thoroughly heated through, adjust seasonings, and then spoon over the scallops. Garnish with a scattering of parsley and, if desired, fried capers.

Substitution: You may use more smoked bacon in place of the speck.

Side Dish Suggestions: Sautéed Swiss Chard with White Anchovies and Lemon Zest; Sautéed Tuscan Black Kale with Speck; Braised Fennel with Tomato and Sambuca

Suggested Wine: Müller-Thurgau or Sylvaner

Scampi alla Griglia con Burro al Limone Grigliato e Parmigiano Reggiano

Grilled Jumbo Shrimp with Charred Lemon Butter, Preserved Chilies, and Parmigiano-Reggiano

It is often said that the Italians absolutely never mix seafood and cheese. One suspects that this purported rule is so often cited as much by virtue of being easy to remember as for any basis in reality. Here is proof that cheese and seafood do mingle well, even in an Italian dish.

Serves 4 as an appetizer or 2 as a main course

3 lemons, halved crosswise
12 jumbo shrimp (about 2 lb/1 kg)
2 tbsp (30 mL) warm clarified butter
½ cup (125 mL) butter, cubed, at room temperature
2 tbsp (30 mL) minced oil-preserved red chilies
1 clove garlic, minced
Leaves from ¼ bunch parsley, chopped
¼ cup (60 mL) freshly grated Parmigiano-Reggiano
Salt and pepper

GARNISH
Crispy-fried parsley (optional; page 278)

Preheat grill on its highest setting. Grill the lemons flesh side down until lightly charred. Juice 2 of them and set aside the third. Butterfly (or have your fishmonger butterfly) the shrimp without severing one half of the shell from the other. Devein them, splay them open flat, and brush lightly with some of the clarified butter. Char buttered side down, brush with clarified butter, and flip them. Just before the shrimp are cooked through, remove them to a large bowl. Add the cubed butter and toss. As the butter melts, add the reserved lemon juice, chilies, garlic, parsley, and Parmesan; keep tossing until the sauce binds and the shrimp are well coated. Season, toss again, and serve on a warm platter with the 2 reserved grilled lemon halves.

Variation: This is a great dish all on its own, but these shrimp make a wonderful accompaniment to a grilled steak.

Suggested Wine: Fiano di Avellino

Scampi Saltati con Borlotti Stufati e Pesto
Sautéed Shrimp with Stewed Borlotti Beans and Pesto

The classic pairing of beans and tuna is more familiar, but this combination of beans and shrimp is as successful, if not more so. Here we sauté the shrimp in fragrant pesto and perch them atop nutty, creamy borlotti beans stewed in sweet shrimp stock and tomato.

Serves 6

1½ cups (325 mL) dried borlotti beans
4 tbsp (60 mL) olive oil
¼ cup (60 mL) julienned prosciutto di Parma
3 tbsp (50 mL) basic soffritto (page 285)
2 cloves garlic, minced
¾ cup (175 mL) white wine
1 can (28 oz/796 mL) San Marzano tomatoes
1 quart (1 L) shrimp stock (page 285), at a simmer
Leaves from ½ bunch basil
1 tbsp (15 mL) minced parsley
2 cloves garlic, crushed
30 medium shrimp (about 2 lb/1 kg), shelled and deveined
Salt and pepper
3 tbsp (50 mL) basil pesto (page 281)

Pick over the beans, and transfer to a bowl. Cover generously with cold water and leave to soak overnight, changing the water 2 or 3 times. Drain and rinse the beans, transfer to a Dutch oven, and cover with cold water. Do not add salt. Bring to a boil, reduce heat and simmer, uncovered, until the beans are tender but not yet losing their skins, about 1 hour. Drain and set aside.

In a saucepan, heat 2 tbsp (30 mL) of the oil on medium-high heat. Add the prosciutto and soffritto; sauté for 2 to 3 minutes. Add the minced garlic and cook 1 minute longer. Deglaze with ¼ cup (60 mL) of the white wine. When that has almost completely evaporated, add the tomatoes, crushing them by hand as you introduce them to the pot. Bring briefly to a boil, and then reduce heat to low. Simmer, uncovered, until the tomatoes thicken substantially, about 25 minutes. Add the beans, shrimp stock, basil, and parsley; stir. Simmer, uncovered, for another 20 minutes.

In a large skillet, sauté the crushed garlic cloves in the remaining 2 tbsp (30 mL) olive oil until golden. Add the shrimp, season with salt and pepper, and cook until medium-rare. Add the remaining ½ cup (125 mL) white wine and reduce by two-thirds. Stir in the pesto.

Season the beans. Ladle into 6 warm shallow bowls. Arrange 5 shrimp on top of each portion. Spoon the pesto from the shrimp pan over top, and serve.

Suggested Wine: Vernaccia

Sgombro Scottato con Peperoni Arrosti e Zafferano
Seared Mackerel Fillets with Roasted Peppers and Saffron

The mackerel, which is plentiful on both our east and west coasts, is a largely ignored commodity in North America. To understand why the opposite is true in Europe, try this dish, wherein the oily flesh of the fish is paired with the perfect agrodolce counterpoint of sweet peppers and a tangy sauce infused with vinegar and saffron. **Serves 4**

2 red and 2 yellow bell peppers, charred and peeled
1 tsp (5 mL) plus 2 tbsp (30 mL) sugar
1 tbsp (15 mL) chopped parsley
Pinch of chili flakes
Salt and black pepper
4 tbsp (60 mL) olive oil
1 cup (250 mL) minced leek (white part only)
1½ cups (375 mL) white wine vinegar
2 tbsp (30 mL) lemon juice
1 tbsp (15 mL) minced thyme
2 cloves garlic, thinly sliced
8 saffron threads, crushed
½ cup (125 mL) fine olive oil
4 mackerel fillets (each about 5 oz/150 g)

Seed and then julienne the bell peppers. Combine in a bowl with 1 tsp (5 mL) of the sugar, and the parsley and chili flakes. Season with salt and pepper, toss, and set aside.

Heat 2 tbsp (30 mL) of the olive oil in a sauté pan over the lowest possible heat. Add the leek and sweat gently until completely wilted, about 10 minutes. Add the white wine vinegar and lemon juice, raise the heat, and bring to a simmer. Stir in the remaining 2 tbsp (30 mL) sugar, and the thyme, garlic, and saffron. Season lightly, and reduce by half. Whisk in the fine olive oil, and keep warm.

Massage the mackerel fillets with a little of the remaining 2 tbsp (30 mL) olive oil. Season well on both sides. In a nonstick skillet over medium-high, heat the remaining olive oil. Add the mackerel skin side down. When after about 90 seconds the skin is crisp and golden at the edges, flip the fish, and cook until done, about 90 seconds more. Remove from the pan and let rest for 2 minutes.

To serve, toss the peppers once more, and mound them at the centre of 4 warm plates. Perch a mackerel fillet skin side up against the peppers. Whisk the warm leek and saffron sauce once more, and drizzle all around the fish.

Suggested Wine: Prosecco

Pesce Spada alla Griglia con Finocchio e Arancia
Grilled Swordfish with Fennel and Orange

Swordfish is, like tuna, a staple of Sicilian cuisine—in which it is most frequently paired with another locally sourced essential, the caper berry. Here instead we match it with another Mediterranean mainstay—fennel—and brighten the mix with citrus. This is a perfect summer dish. **Serves 4**

4 swordfish loin steaks (each about 5 oz/150 g)
½ cup (125 mL) Roasted Garlic Dressing (page 27)
2 medium fennel bulbs
3 tbsp (50 mL) olive oil
1 tsp (5 mL) sugar
Salt and pepper
Juice of 2 oranges
¼ cup (60 mL) aged wine vinegar
1 tbsp (15 mL) liquid honey
1 tsp (5 mL) toasted fennel seeds, crushed
2 cups (500 mL) fish stock (page 286)

GARNISH
1 orange
1 cup (250 mL) shaved fennel
¼ cup (60 mL) fennel fronds
1 tbsp (15 mL) chopped parsley
½ tsp (2 mL) minced oregano
2 tbsp (30 mL) fine olive oil
Salt and pepper

Turn the fish in the garlic dressing to coat, then set aside to marinate on the countertop for 30 minutes, turning once midway.

Meanwhile, trim the stalks and fronds from the fennel bulbs. Halve each bulb lengthwise, and then cut each half into 3 wedges, keeping enough of the core intact to hold each wedge together. Transfer to a large bowl and toss with 1 tbsp (15 mL) of the olive oil, the sugar, and salt and pepper. Heat a large sauté pan on medium-high. Add the remaining 2 tbsp (30 mL) olive oil, and just before it smokes, carefully add the fennel wedges, jostling them with a wooden spoon so that they sit flat on their sides in maximum contact with the scorching-hot pan. When one side is bronzed, turn and repeat. When the second side is caramelized, add the orange juice, vinegar, honey, and fennel seeds. Stir gently. When the liquid thickens and has reduced by half, add the stock. Bring to a boil, lower heat to a simmer, and partly cover the pan. Braise until the fennel is tender, about 20 minutes.

Preheat grill on high.

Shake the excess marinade from the swordfish steaks, and season with salt and pepper. Oil the grill. Grill the fish to medium doneness, and then set aside to rest for 2 minutes. Meanwhile, for the garnish, peel the orange; working over a bowl to capture its juices, cut out the orange segments from between their membranes. To the orange segments and juice in the bowl, add the shaved fennel, fennel fronds, parsley, oregano, and half the fine olive oil. Season, and toss briefly.

Arrange 3 braised fennel segments at the centre of each of 4 warm plates and drizzle generously with their braising liquid. Place a swordfish steak on top of the braised fennel, and then mound a handful of the fennel and orange salad on top of each portion of fish. Drizzle with remaining fine olive oil, and serve.

Substitution: If fish stock is unavailable, use chicken stock (page 286), but not *brodo*, for its flavour is too assertive.

Suggested Wine: Dolcetto

Carne Meat

Porchetta con Mostarda di Pere
Slow-Roasted Pork Shoulder with Pear Mostarda

Porchetta traditionally comprises a whole pork loin and belly, but roasting only the shoulder is definitely more practical in the home kitchen. The shoulder is arguably the tastiest cut of the pig—and when it is coated with this fragrant rub and slow roasted, definitively so.

Serves 8 to 10

20 sage leaves, minced
Leaves from 3 sprigs thyme, minced
Leaves from 3 sprigs rosemary, minced
2 cloves garlic, minced
1 tsp (5 mL) toasted fennel seeds, ground
1 boneless skin-on pork shoulder (about 6 lb/2.7 kg)
2 tbsp (30 mL) olive oil

Salt and cracked black pepper
½ cup (125 mL) white wine
1 tbsp (15 mL) cornstarch, dissolved in cold water
1 tsp (5 mL) aged wine vinegar
½ cup (125 mL) oregano pesto (page 281)
1 batch pear mostarda (see page 211)

Preheat oven to 275°F (140°C).

In a small bowl, combine the sage, thyme, rosemary, garlic, and fennel seeds; mix well. Rub the pork with the olive oil and season it generously with salt and pepper. Sprinkle with the rub on all sides, pressing it lightly into the meat. Arrange the pork skin side up and score the skin in a grid without cutting all the way through to the meat. Now flip the meat over. If it does not sit relatively flat, carefully butterfly the section that bulges. Roll the pork as tightly as possible, in such a way that the skin ends up fully exposed on the outside. Tie it snugly with butcher's twine. Place the pork on a rack in a roasting pan, and loosely tent with foil. Transfer to the oven and roast, basting every 30 minutes or so, for about 6 hours—until a meat thermometer inserted into the thickest part of the cut registers 165°F (75°C). Transfer pork to a cutting board.

Pour the excess fat from the roasting pan. Place over high heat. Add the wine and stir vigorously to free all the drippings stuck to the bottom of the pan. When they appear to be fully dissolved, pass through a sieve into a saucepan. Bring to a simmer over medium-low heat, whisk in the cornstarch mixture, and simmer for 2 minutes. Taste and adjust seasonings. Adjust acidity to taste with the vinegar, adding only a few drops at a time (and without necessarily using all of it).

Break away the crackling and slice the pork to desired thickness. Serve pork slices drizzled with the pan juices and dabbed with pesto, and with a dollop of pear mostarda and crackling on the side.

Side Dish Suggestions: Roast Potatoes with Rosemary and Garlic; Roman Cauliflower with Cheese Sauce; Sautéed Tuscan Black Kale with Speck; Spring Peas with Carrots and Rabbit Sauce; Grilled Radicchio di Treviso with Balsamic Dressing

Suggested Wine: Chianti Classico or Aglianico

Brasato di Pancia di Maiale con Mele Caramelizzate
Braised Pork Belly with Caramelized Apples

It is hard to think of a cut of meat more luscious than a properly braised slice of pork belly. To achieve a result that is both flawlessly tender and permeated with aromatic flavour, we recommend brining the meat for two days before slowly braising it. Serves 6

½ cup (125 mL) kosher salt
½ cup (125 mL) brown sugar
6 cloves garlic, smashed
1 tbsp (15 mL) plus 1 tsp (5 mL) black peppercorns
¼ bunch oregano
2 sprigs rosemary
8 bay leaves
3 lb (1.5 kg) pork belly, skin on
3 tbsp (50 mL) olive oil
1 medium Spanish onion, sliced
½ fennel bulb, sliced
2 quarts (2 L) pork stock (page 286)
¼ cup (60 mL) vegetable oil
2 cups (500 mL) sweet apple cider
1 tbsp (15 mL) clarified butter
3 Granny Smith apples, peeled, cored, and cut into eighths or cubed
1 tsp (5 mL) sugar
Generous pinch of ground cinnamon
1 tbsp (15 mL) butter

GARNISH
18 crispy-fried sage leaves (optional; page 278)

In a Dutch oven large enough to hold the pork snugly, combine the salt, sugar, garlic, 1 tbsp (15 mL) of the peppercorns, oregano, rosemary, 6 of the bay leaves, and 5 cups (1.25 L) cold water. Bring to a boil, reduce heat, and simmer, stirring, until the salt and sugar dissolve. Then chill. Once cooled, completely submerge the pork in the brine (add cold water if necessary to cover). Cover and refrigerate for 2 days.

Preheat oven to 325°F (160°C).

Remove the pork from the brine (discarding the brine), rinse under cold running water, and pat dry. Heat the olive oil in a large sauté pan on medium heat, and then sweat the onion and fennel until wilted. Add the remaining 1 tsp (5 mL) peppercorns and 2 bay leaves and the pork. Add pork stock to cover, bring to a simmer, cover, and transfer to the oven. Check the stock level periodically and top it up if evaporation leaves the pork exposed. After 2½ hours test the pork for tenderness. If it does not yet yield easily when prodded with a fork, continue to braise, testing every 30 minutes until the meat is very tender.

Remove the pork from the braising liquid and transfer to a baking sheet to cool. Strain the braising liquid into a saucepan. Cover the pork with a sheet of parchment paper, then with a second baking sheet, and add weight (bricks, tins of tomatoes, cans of beer, what have you). Transfer pork and braising liquid to the refrigerator overnight.

Preheat oven to 400°F (200°C).

Remove and discard the skin from the pork; cut the pork into 6 equal portions. Remove and discard the hardened fat from the surface of the braising liquid. Bring the liquid to a boil and reduce to desired intensity. Lower the heat to a simmer, and adjust seasonings.

Heat the vegetable oil in a skillet on medium-high. Working in batches if necessary, brown the pork belly portions on all sides. Transfer the pork to the oven for 20 minutes. Meanwhile, bring the apple cider to a boil and reduce to about ½ cup (125 mL).

In a large nonstick skillet on medium-high, melt the butter. Add the apples, sprinkle them with sugar, and lightly caramelize on both sides. Sprinkle with cinnamon and douse with the apple cider syrup.

To serve, arrange portions of pork in the middle of 6 warm plates. Spoon apples and their syrup over top. Whisk the butter into the pork reduction and drizzle 1 tbsp (15 mL) around the edge of each plate. Garnish with crispy sage leaves if desired.

Substitutions: Peaches serve just as nicely as apples as a sweet and acidic counterpoint to the fatty pork. Prepare them in the same way, but reduce peach nectar in place of the apple juice, and season them with a pinch of star anise powder in place of the cinnamon.

Side Dish Suggestions: Roasted Beets with Pistachios and Balsamic Vinegar; Sweet-and-Sour Squash

Suggested Wine: Fiano di Avellino or Barbera d'Asti

Bistecca alla Fiorentina
Char-Grilled Porterhouse with Grilled Lemon and Roasted Garlic

This legendary steak of Tuscany has things going for it that we simply cannot replicate. Clippings from an old Sangiovese vine with which to stoke your grill fire are hard to come by here. So is their breed of beef. And even if you do manage to locate a semi-local herd of Chianina—as we did for Fabbrica—you will not find a slaughterhouse equipped to handle its awesome heft. So we instead focus here on making local beef taste as Tuscan as it can.

Serves 4

2 heads garlic
¼ cup (60 mL) olive oil
Salt and pepper
2 grass-fed PEI Black Angus (or other top-quality) porterhouse steaks (each about 2 lb/1 kg)
2 tbsp (30 mL) minced rosemary

2 tbsp (30 mL) minced parsley
1 tbsp (15 mL) minced sage
1 tbsp (15 mL) minced garlic
1 lemon, halved crosswise
Fine olive oil

Preheat oven to 300°F (150°C).

Cut off and discard the top ½ inch (1 cm) from each head of garlic. Arrange them at the centre of a sheet of foil, drizzle lightly with some of the olive oil, season, and seal snugly. Roast until tender, about 1 hour. Set aside.

Massage the steaks with 1 tbsp (15 mL) of the olive oil and season them very generously with salt and (preferably cracked) pepper. In a small bowl, combine the rosemary, parsley, sage, and minced garlic with the remaining olive oil. Mix well and then rub all over the steaks. Set steaks aside on the counter for 20 minutes.

Meanwhile, preheat grill on its highest setting. Grill the lemon flesh side down until lightly charred, and set aside. Char the steaks for about 3 minutes a side and then shift to a more temperate area of the grill until cooked to desired doneness. Remove to a carving board, cover loosely with foil, and let rest for 10 minutes. Cut the strip loins and tenderloins from their bones. Slice the beef perpendicular to its length into strips about ¼ inch (5 mm) thick, and then reassemble the steaks around the T-bones on a warm platter. Drizzle lightly with the fine olive oil and serve with the roasted garlic and grilled lemon.

Substitutions: Any quality, well-marbled beef can serve as a substitute for our favoured grass-fed Blue Dot steaks from PEI. But do attempt to seek out beef that was at least partially dry-aged. Wet-aged beef from the supermarket will shrink considerably during cooking, rendering this grand dish anemic.

Tip: Salt is not generally included in a marinade for meat or fish, as it extracts moisture from the flesh. But you need not fear any such effect taking place over a mere 20 minutes on the countertop.

Side Dish Suggestions: Risotto with Roast Marrow and Veal *Jus*; Roast Potatoes with Rosemary and Garlic; Grilled Radicchio di Treviso with Balsamic Dressing; Grilled Asparagus

Suggested Wine: Chianti Classico or Brunello

Costolette di Manzo con Polenta
Braised Short Ribs with Polenta

Braised short ribs arrived on high-end menus just over a decade ago, and because of their nearly incomparable combination of tenderness and flavour, they were quickly entrenched as a popular favourite that was here to stay. Here we serve them on the creamy backdrop of polenta, with dabs of tomato passato providing a necessary jolt of acidity. **Serves 6**

6 pieces short rib, cut 3 inches (7 cm) wide
    (about 3 lb/1.5 kg)
⅓ cup (75 mL) olive oil
Salt and coarsely ground pepper
1 large Spanish onion, chopped
1 cup (250 mL) chopped carrots
1 stalk celery, chopped
6 cloves garlic, smashed
2 ripe Roma tomatoes, cored and quartered
2 sprigs thyme
1 sprig rosemary
2 bay leaves
1 cup (250 mL) white wine
1 quart (1 L) *brodo* (page 3)
1 batch polenta (see page 68)
¼ cup (60 mL) tomato passato (page 83)
¼ cup (60 mL) chopped or crispy-fried parsley
    (page 278)
Fine olive oil

Preheat oven to 325°F (160°C).

Massage the short ribs with some of the olive oil and season them generously with salt and pepper. Set a pot large enough to accommodate the ribs in a single layer over medium-high heat, and heat 2 tbsp (30 mL) of the olive oil. Brown the short ribs on all sides, about 10 minutes. Remove to a platter.

Pour off most of the fat. Reduce heat to medium-low and add the remaining 2 tbsp (30 mL) olive oil. Add the onions and salt them lightly. Sweat the onions until translucent. Add the carrots, celery, garlic, tomatoes, and herbs; sweat, stirring regularly—do not let the vegetables brown. When the vegetables have softened, deglaze with the wine, and reduce the wine by half. Return the short ribs to the pot. Add enough *brodo* to cover, bring to a simmer, cover, and transfer to the oven.

Check the short ribs after 1½ hours, turning them if they are not completely covered with liquid. Expect a cooking time between 3 and 4 hours, but test for tenderness after 2½ hours—and every half hour after that. The meat should be pulling away from the bone and yield easily when pierced with a fork.

When the short ribs are done, transfer to a cutting board. Cutting as close to the bone as possible, remove the cap of beef from the bone beneath. Discard the bones and the cartilaginous matter that joins them. Cut each portion of beef into 2 or 3 large pieces. Transfer the meat to a small pot, set a strainer over top, and pour in just enough braising liquid to cover. Strain the rest of the braising liquid into another pot, pushing a little of the cooked vegetables through the sieve, if desired. Reduce the sauce by about half, or until it attains the desired consistency. Adjust seasonings, and set aside.

Meanwhile, prepare the polenta, finishing it with butter, salt, and pepper. Distribute the polenta among 6 warm plates (or spread on a serving platter). Drizzle it with the sauce, and arrange beef pieces to one side. Douse the beef with more sauce, dab with passato, scatter with parsley, and drizzle with olive oil.

Substitutions: You may prepare the polenta with chicken stock (page 286) or vegetable stock in place of the *brodo*. Even water will do in a pinch.

Side Dish Suggestions: Roasted Beets with Pistachios and Balsamic Vinegar; Grilled Radicchio di Treviso with Balsamic Dressing; Sweet-and-Sour Squash

Suggested Wine: Montepulciano d'Abruzzo or Vino Nobile di Montepulciano

Vitello alla Griglia con Porcini e Panna
Grilled Veal Chops with Porcini Cream Sauce

The veal chop became popular in North American restaurants in the 1980s, concurrent with a trend for cooking things more lightly, and the result was that to its great detriment a lot of veal is still cooked as if it were tuna. Do not do this. Veal is not beef—served rare, it has the texture of old chewing gum. A veal chop shows best when cooked medium. **Serves 6**

4 tbsp (60 mL) olive oil
2 tbsp (30 mL) minced rosemary
2 tbsp (30 mL) minced parsley
2 tbsp (30 mL) minced sage
2 tbsp (30 mL) minced thyme
1 tbsp (15 mL) cracked black pepper
1 tbsp (15 mL) minced garlic
6 veal rib chops (each about 10 oz/300 g)
Salt
3 tbsp (50 mL) minced onion

1 clove garlic, minced
½ cup (125 mL) Pinot Grigio
3 cups (750 mL) porcini mushrooms,
    sliced ¼ inch (5 mm) thick
Salt and pepper
¾ cup (175 mL) 35% cream
¼ cup (60 mL) freshly grated Parmigiano-Reggiano
Squeeze of lemon juice
6 sprigs thyme for garnish

Preheat grill on high.

In a small bowl, combine 3 tbsp (50 mL) of the olive oil with the rosemary, parsley, sage, thyme, pepper, and garlic; mix well. Rub the mixture all over the veal chops, and then salt them generously. Place the chops on the grill and sear for 3 minutes on each side, then lower the heat to medium and cook for 5 or 6 minutes more on each side or until medium doneness. Transfer to a plate, tent loosely with foil, and let rest for 10 minutes.

Meanwhile, in a large sauté pan, sweat the onion in the remaining 1 tbsp (15 mL) olive oil until wilted. Add the garlic and sweat a minute longer. Add the white wine, raise the heat, and reduce by two-thirds. Add the mushrooms, season with salt and pepper, and cook until wilted. Add the cream and reduce by one-third. Taste, and correct the seasonings. Stir in the Parmesan, 1 tbsp (15 mL) at a time, until the sauce is smooth. To finish, stir in a squeeze of lemon juice.

Place 1 chop on each of 6 warm plates, pour the sauce over top, and garnish with a sprig of thyme.

Substitutions: Any top-quality mushroom can stand in for the porcini: morels, for example, would be just as good. If you use dried mushrooms instead of fresh, Italian-packaged porcini are usually sold in envelopes of 20 g (0.7 oz)—two of those will suffice for this recipe. Soak the dried mushrooms for an hour in warm water. Strain the liquid and add along with the mushrooms—but reduce thoroughly before adding the cream.

Side Dish Suggestions: Roast Potatoes with Rosemary and Garlic; Spring Peas with Carrots and Rabbit Sauce

Suggested Wine: Barbaresco

Vitello in Bianco con Gremolata di Rafano
Poached Veal with Horseradish Gremolata

Poaching veal in a good broth at gentle simmer on the stovetop yields an unfailingly tender, moist, and flavoursome result. The rub we use is fragrant, but not assertive. Do take care to sear the veal only lightly before poaching it, as anything more will burn the herbs and adversely affect the final flavour. **Serves 8**

10 sage leaves, minced
Leaves from 3 sprigs oregano, minced
Leaves from 3 sprigs thyme, minced
Leaves from 1 sprig rosemary, minced
2 cloves garlic, minced
1 tsp (5 mL) toasted fennel seeds, ground
½ tsp (2 mL) combined minced lemon and orange zest
¼ cup (60 mL) olive oil
1 veal brisket (about 5 lb/2.2 kg)
Salt and cracked black pepper
3 quarts (3 L) *brodo* (page 3), at a simmer
1 batch horseradish gremolata (page 278)

In a small bowl, combine the sage, oregano, thyme, rosemary, garlic, fennel seeds, and zests; mix well. Rub the brisket with 2 tbsp (30 mL) of the oil and season it generously with salt and pepper. Sprinkle with the rub on all sides, pressing it lightly into the meat. Fold the pointed end of the brisket back toward its centre. Beginning at the folded end, tightly roll up the brisket. Tie the roll together securely with butcher's twine.

Heat the remaining 2 tbsp (30 mL) olive oil in a large skillet on medium-high, and then sear the brisket on all sides—but lightly, so as not to burn the herbs. Transfer the brisket to an oval Dutch oven just large enough to accommodate the roll. Pour in enough *brodo* to cover, and bring to a boil over medium-high heat. Immediately reduce the heat, cover, and simmer, turning the brisket periodically, until the meat is tender and yields easily when pierced with a fork, about 3 hours.

Remove the brisket to a platter, cover loosely with foil, and let it rest for 15 minutes. Meanwhile, skim the fat from the poaching liquid, then strain it into a sauté pan. Reduce over high heat by half, or until desired intensity and consistency. Slice the brisket about ½ inch (1 cm) thick and arrange it on a warm platter. Drizzle with the reduced poaching liquid, and then scatter the gremolata over top.

Side Dish Suggestions: Risotto with Mushrooms and Shaved Truffle; Roast Potatoes with Rosemary and Garlic; Sautéed Tuscan Black Kale with Speck; Spring Peas with Carrots and Rabbit Sauce

Suggested Wine: Dolcetto or Valpolicella

Brasato di Collo d'Agnello con Salsiccia d'Agnello e Caponata
Braised Lamb Neck with Lamb Sausage and Caponata

When properly braised, the meat drawn from the neck of the lamb is incomparably tender and sweet. It lends itself well to a ragù, or to filling ravioli. Here, though, we showcase it in its rustic glory, serving it on the bone like a piece of osso buco. The sausage adds heartiness to the plate, and the lightly vinegared caponata provides a necessary acidic counterpoint.

Serves 8

8 slices lamb neck (each 1½ inches/4 cm and about 8 oz/250 g)
½ cup (125 mL) olive oil
Salt and pepper
1 large Spanish onion, chopped
½ large fennel bulb, core and fronds removed, sliced
4 cloves garlic, sliced
Leaves from ½ bunch basil

6 sprigs parsley
1 sprig mint
2 cups (500 mL) white wine
1 can (28 oz/796 mL) San Marzano tomatoes
2 quarts (2 L) *brodo* (page 3), at a simmer
8 lamb sausages (page 279)
1 batch caponata (page 276)

Pat the lamb pieces dry with a paper towel. Rub them with about 2 tbsp (30 mL) of the olive oil, and season them generously with salt and pepper. In a large Dutch oven on medium-high, heat ¼ cup (60 mL) of the olive oil. Working in batches if necessary, add the lamb and sear it until nicely bronzed on all sides. Remove the lamb to a platter, pour off the fat from the pot, and return it to the heat.

Heat the remaining 2 tbsp (30 mL) olive oil. Add the onions and fennel. Sauté until they begin to wilt, about 3 minutes. Add the garlic and sauté it for 2 minutes, stirring vigorously to prevent it from acquiring colour. Add the basil, parsley, and mint. Return the lamb and its juices to the pot and then deglaze with the white wine. When that has reduced to a syrup, add the tomatoes. Finally, add enough hot *brodo* to cover the lamb (you may not need all of it). Bring to a boil, reduce to a simmer, cover, and cook gently until the meat is tender and yields easily when pierced with a fork, about 2 hours.

Remove the lamb to a platter and cover loosely with foil. Discard the herb sprigs, and buzz the sauce in a blender (or with a hand blender). Reduce if desired. Adjust seasonings and return the lamb to the pot to reheat. Meanwhile, fry or grill the sausages and reheat the caponata. Serve from the table, dousing each slice of lamb with sauce.

Substitutions: While our lamb sausage recipe is particularly rewarding, it is completely understandable that you may not wish to take the trouble to prepare a batch. Note that we make short, 3-inch (7 cm) links, and so if you purchase yours from the butcher, you will need 4 sausages—one half-sausage per portion.

Suggested Wine: Brunello or Tuscan IGT

Crespelle di Capra con Ricotta e Soffritto
Goat Crêpes with Ricotta and Soffritto

Young goat (*capretto*) is a popular snack from the mountainous regions of Italy to Asia, and from the Caribbean to Central and South America. In North America, meanwhile, the animal remains more of a curiosity than a dietary staple. This is a pity, because goat is not just extremely flavourful but also the leanest, healthiest meat one can consume. **Makes 12 crêpes**

4 eggs
2 cups (500 mL) milk
1½ cups (375 mL) all-purpose flour
½ tsp (2 mL) salt
¼ cup (60 mL) butter, melted
3 tbsp (50 mL) olive oil
2 lb (1 kg) goat leg or shoulder,
    cut into 1½-inch (4 cm) cubes
Salt and pepper
3 cloves garlic, chopped
2 sprigs rosemary
2-inch (5 cm) piece cinnamon stick

½ star anise
Pinch of chili flakes
1 cup (250 mL) white wine
1 can (28 oz/796 mL) San Marzano tomatoes
2 quarts (2 L) *brodo* (page 3), at a simmer
1 cup (250 mL) buffalo ricotta,
    drained in cheesecloth for 24 hours
1 cup (250 mL) basic soffritto (page 285)

GARNISH
Freshly grated pecorino
2 tbsp (30 mL) fine olive oil

The day before serving, prepare the crêpe batter. In a large bowl, beat the eggs. Whisk in the milk, and follow with the flour, salt, and melted butter; whisk until smooth. Pass through a fine-mesh sieve into a sealable container, and set aside in the refrigerator overnight.

To prepare the goat, heat the oil in a large saucepan or Dutch oven on medium-high heat. Add the meat, season generously, and brown well on all sides. Stir in the garlic, rosemary, cinnamon, star anise, and chili flakes. Deglaze with the white wine. When the wine has reduced to a syrup, add the tomatoes and lower the heat. Add just enough *brodo* to cover the meat. Simmer, partially covered, until the meat is tender, about 2½ hours. Remove and discard herb stems, cinnamon stick, and star anise. With a slotted spoon transfer the goat pieces to a bowl or platter, cover loosely with foil, and let cool for about 15 minutes. While it is still warm, shred the meat and pick over it carefully, removing all bones. Stir the sauce, crush the tomatoes, and adjust the seasonings; set aside 1 cup (250 mL) of the sauce. Return the shredded goat to the pot. Fold in the ricotta. Set aside.

Preheat oven to 375°F (180°C). Heat a 7-inch (18 cm) nonstick skillet on medium-low. Add 3 tbsp (50 mL) of the batter to the dry pan and cook like a pancake until golden on both sides, about 1 minute total. Repeat until you have 12 crêpes. Scatter the soffritto over the bottom of a casserole dish. Spoon about ¼ cup (60 mL) of the goat filling in a strip down the middle of each crêpe, then roll them up like cylinders; arrange them in a row on top of the soffritto. Pour the reserved goat sauce over the crêpes and transfer to the oven. Bake, basting the crêpes every 5 minutes, until they are heated through and lightly bronzed, about 25 minutes. Garnish with grated pecorino and fine olive oil.

Tip: If the goat mixture is hot rather than warm, the filling will be too runny to use to fill the crêpes. And if it is chilled, it will not be properly heated through in the 20-odd minutes required to bake the crêpes.

Suggested Wine: Nero d'Avola or lighter Primitivo

Animelle Fritte alla Marsala
Crisp-Fried Sweetbreads with Marsala

In English Canada, sweetbreads are seldom seen on display at the butcher shop, and even those people who jump at the chance to eat them at a good restaurant tend to forget to place a special advance order so that they can make them at home. This is a shame, because they are extremely easy to prepare. **Serves 4**

1 quart (1 L) veal stock (page 286)
4 sprigs parsley
1 sprig thyme
1 bay leaf
2 lb (1 kg) sweetbreads
2 eggs
1 cup (250 mL) milk
Flour for dredging
Salt and pepper
2 cups fresh bread crumbs
1 tbsp (15 mL) combined minced thyme, parsley,
    sage, and oregano
2 cups (500 mL) olive oil

2 tbsp (30 mL) minced onion
1 cup (250 mL) chanterelles or other top-quality
    mushroom, trimmed and sliced
¼ cup (60 mL) dry Marsala
⅓ cup (75 mL) *brodo* (page 3)
2 tbsp (30 mL) capers, rinsed and drained
1 tbsp (15 mL) minced parsley
1 tbsp (15 mL) butter
Squeeze of lemon juice

GARNISH
Crispy-fried parsley (optional; page 278)

Bring the veal stock to a boil, add the parsley sprigs, thyme, and bay leaf, and lower heat to a simmer. Add the sweetbreads and poach until medium-rare, about 5 minutes. Shock in a bath of ice water, then drain. Pat dry with paper towels. Carefully peel the membrane from the sweetbreads with the aid of a sharp knife, then wrap them individually in plastic wrap and transfer to a large casserole. Place a smaller dish on top, weight it with tins of tomatoes or the like, and transfer to the refrigerator overnight.

Unwrap the sweetbreads and slice them into scaloppine about ½ inch (1 cm) thick. In a shallow dish, beat together the eggs and milk. In 2 separate shallow dishes, season the flour and combine the minced herbs with the bread crumbs.

To begin the sauce, in a medium skillet, sweat the onion in 1 tbsp (15 mL) olive oil until wilted. Add the mushrooms and raise the heat to medium. When the mushrooms have wilted and released their liquid, add the Marsala and *brodo*. Reduce by half.

Meanwhile, heat the remaining olive oil in a skillet on medium-high. Dredge the sweetbreads in the flour, dip them in the egg mixture, then coat them with the bread crumbs. Fry until golden and crisp, about 2 minutes per side. Remove to a warm platter to rest while you finish the sauce by stirring in the capers, minced parsley, butter, and lemon juice. Season to taste. Arrange the sweetbreads on a warm platter and pour the sauce over top. If you so choose, garnish with fried parsley.

Substitution: If you don't have veal stock, simply poach the sweetbreads in salted water.

Side Dish Suggestion: Roast Potatoes with Rosemary and Garlic

Suggested Wine: young Chianti

Pollastrello Arrosto con Passato di Pomodoro
Pan-Roasted Baby Chicken with Tomato Passato

A young, tender chicken—of the sort your butcher likely labels a broiler—lends itself particularly well to pan-roasting. When it is boned and pressed as described, its skin will be flawlessly crisp and its flesh supple and succulent. This makes a perfect roast for two—but of course, you can easily multiply the recipe to serve as many as you please. **Serves 2**

¼ cup (60 mL) sugar
1 sprig rosemary
1 small chicken (about 2½ lb/1.25 kg)
3 tbsp (50 mL) olive oil
Salt and pepper

1 tbsp (15 mL) top-quality red wine vinegar
2 tbsp (30 mL) butter
2 tbsp (30 mL) puréed tomato passato (page 83)
1 tbsp (15 mL) fine olive oil

Preheat oven to 325°F (160°C).

Combine the sugar with an equal amount of water in a small saucepan, and heat, stirring, until completely dissolved. Dip the rosemary in the simple syrup and then place it on a rack on a baking sheet. Bake for 5 minutes and then set aside to dry for about 2 hours.

Preheat oven to 375°F (190°C).

Bone (or ask your butcher to bone) the chicken in such a way that the bird is halved and only the lower wing and leg bones (and not the thigh bones) remain. Slash the leg ¼ inch (5 mm) deep 3 times on each side (optional). Massage the bird with half of the olive oil and season it generously. Heat a large nonstick skillet over medium-high heat. Add the chicken halves skin side down, place a second, smaller skillet (or a brick) on top to weight them down, and sear until bronzed, about 7 minutes. Transfer the weighted bird to the oven and roast for 10 minutes. Remove the weight, flip the halves, and baste. Return to the oven until fully cooked, about another 5 minutes. Transfer to 2 warm serving plates (or a warm platter).

Pour off any excess fat from the skillet and place it over medium-high heat. Deglaze the pan with the vinegar, and then stir in the butter until melted. Season lightly and pour the sauce around the chicken. Dab each half of the bird with the passato and then crumble rosemary leaves over top. Drizzle with the fine olive oil and serve.

Substitutions: This same preparation works just as well with Cornish Rock hens, but you will need an entire bird for each serving. If you wish, you may skip toasting the rosemary and instead snip a little of its leaves into the roasting pan before adding the bird. The aesthetic will not be as pleasing, but the flavour will be just as good.

Side Dish Suggestions: Deep-Fried Baby Artichokes; Grilled Asparagus; Spring Peas with Carrots and Rabbit Sauce

Suggested Wine: Chianti Classico

Pollo alla Parmigiana
Chicken Parmigiana

Some popular dishes are so far removed from the good idea with which they originated that it seldom occurs to a discerning consumer that there was ever actually a good idea there in the first place. But usually there was, and few dishes make the case for this truism more than does this perfectly executed version of that frequently botched American Italian cliché, chicken parmigiana. **Serves 6**

1 batch basic tomato sauce (page 82)
6 boneless, skinless chicken breasts (each about 6 oz/175 g)
3 eggs
Flour for dredging
3 cups (750 mL) fresh bread crumbs
Salt and pepper
4 tbsp (60 mL) clarified butter
4 tbsp (60 mL) olive oil
2 balls mozzarella di bufala (each 4 oz/125 g), cubed
1 cup (250 mL) freshly grated Parmigiano-Reggiano
Fine olive oil
Leaves from ½ bunch basil, torn

Preheat oven to 450°F (230°C). Bring the tomato sauce to a gentle simmer; keep warm.

Arrange the chicken breasts on a cutting board, skin side down. Trim off any excess fat or cartilage. Fold the small tenderloin outward, and if the breasts are especially stout, butterfly them at the thickest part. Place each breast between 2 sheets of plastic wrap. With a meat mallet, pound to an even thickness of about ½ inch (1 cm).

In a shallow dish, lightly beat the eggs. Put the flour and bread crumbs in 2 other shallow dishes. Season the flour and bread crumbs generously with salt and pepper.

Heat 2 large nonstick skillets on medium-high heat (or work in batches in 1 pan). Dredge the cutlets in the flour, then dip them in the egg, letting the excess drip off. Finally, coat them in the bread crumbs. Add 2 tbsp (30 mL) of the clarified butter and 2 tbsp (30 mL) of the oil to each pan, and follow quickly with 3 cutlets in each. Cook until the cutlets are bronzed and crisp on the bottom, about 4 minutes, then flip them. Dot the cooked side of each cutlet with about 2 tbsp (30 mL) of mozzarella. Transfer both pans to the oven and bake until the chicken is cooked through and the cheese is melted, about 6 minutes.

Spread about ¼ cup (60 mL) of the hot tomato sauce in a large circle on each of 4 warm plates. Place 1 cutlet on top, with the melted mozzarella upward. Sprinkle each plate with the Parmesan. Follow with a generous drizzle of fine olive oil and a sprinkling of basil leaves.

Side Dish Suggestions: Roast Potatoes with Rosemary and Garlic; Roasted Beets with Pistachios and Balsamic Vinegar

Suggested Wine: Chianti Classico

Quaglia Affumicata con Mostarda di Albicocche
Smoked Quail with Apricot Mostarda

It is not absolutely essential to go to the trouble of cold-smoking the quail before searing or grilling them—but it is highly recommended. **Serves 4**

8 quail (about 3 lb/1.5 kg total)
1 cup (250 mL) wood chips, soaked
½ tbsp (7 mL) clarified butter
4 firm apricots, each cut into eighths
3 tbsp (50 mL) granulated sugar
1 shallot, minced
½ tbsp (7 mL) minced fresh ginger
½ stick cinnamon
3 tbsp (50 mL) white wine vinegar

1 tsp (5 mL) hot dry mustard
1 tsp (5 mL) Dijon mustard
1 tsp (5 mL) plus ¼ cup (60 mL) butter
Salt and pepper
1 tbsp (15 mL) olive oil
½ tbsp (7 mL) white balsamic vinegar

GARNISH
Crispy-fried sage (optional; page 278)

Cut (or ask your butcher to cut) the legs and thighs from the quail and then bone the breasts, trimming the attached wings to make suprêmes. Load the wood chips into your barbecue according to manufacturer's instructions and smoke the quail pieces at the lowest possible temperature for 20 to 30 minutes. Set the quail aside in the refrigerator.

Melt the clarified butter in a saucepan over medium heat and then add the apricots. When the fruit is heated through, gently stir in the sugar. Once that has dissolved, stir in the shallot, ginger, and cinnamon. When after 3 or 4 minutes the shallot has begun to wilt, stir in the white wine vinegar and 3 tbsp (50 mL) cold water. Bring to a simmer, lower the heat, and simmer, stirring occasionally, until the mixture thickens almost to a jam, but not so much that the apricot segments break apart, about 5 minutes. Stir in the mustards and 1 tsp (5 mL) of the butter, season with salt and pepper. Cover and keep warm.

Preheat grill on high.

Melt the remaining ¼ cup (60 mL) butter in a small saucepan over medium heat. When it foams, stir in the white balsamic vinegar; set aside. Massage the quail pieces with a little olive oil and season them generously with salt and pepper. Brush the grill with oil, and then, beginning skin side down, grill the quail for about 1 minute per side or to desired doneness. Just before removing quail from the grill, lightly brush the skin side with the balsamic butter. Divide the quail among 4 warm plates and serve with a generous portion of mostarda.

Substitutions: You may prepare the mostarda with 2 peeled pears or peaches in place of the 4 apricots. The quail can be seared in a nonstick skillet with a little olive oil instead of being grilled.

Tip: The mostarda also makes a lovely accompaniment for terrines and other salumi. If you prepare it with that in mind, cook the fruit a few minutes longer, until the segments break apart. Serve no warmer than room temperature.

Side Dish Suggestions: Roasted Beets with Pistachios and Balsamic Vinegar; Grilled Radicchio di Treviso with Balsamic Dressing

Suggested Wine: Barbera or Negroamaro

Brasato di Coniglio con Funghi e Olive
Braised Rabbit with Mushrooms and Olives

The combined smoothness and crisp, fruity citrus notes of your average Pinot Grigio lend something distinctive to this braise that other wines do not reliably replicate. So do buy a bottle exclusively for this dish. When you taste the sauce, you will be grateful. Serves 4

1 rabbit (about 3½ lb/1.6 kg)
Salt and pepper
3 tbsp (50 mL) olive oil
½ Spanish onion, halved lengthwise,
   then thinly sliced crosswise
1½ cups (375 mL) cremini mushrooms,
   sliced ¼ inch (50 mm) thick
½ cup (125 mL) oyster mushrooms,
   sliced ¼ inch (50 mm) thick
3 sprigs thyme
2 sprigs rosemary
1 cup (250 mL) infornate olives, rinsed,
   drained, and pitted
2 large cloves garlic, thinly sliced
2 cups (500 mL) Pinot Grigio
6 cups (1.5 L) rabbit stock (page 287)
2 tbsp (30 mL) chopped parsley

Cut (or ask your butcher to cut) the rabbit into 7 serving pieces (2 hind legs, 2 forelegs, 2 half-saddles, 1 double rack). If you wish, remove the thigh bones. Pull fat from the kidneys and discard. Reserve kidneys along with the liver. (All trimmings can be set aside for stock, or larger pieces, like the belly and neck, can be added to the braising pot for flavour.) Season the rabbit generously.

Heat the oil in a large Dutch oven over medium-high heat. Working in batches if necessary, sear the rabbit on both sides just until golden. Remove the rabbit to a platter. Add the onions, mushrooms, thyme, rosemary, and reserved kidneys and liver to the hot fat in the pan. Sauté for about 3 minutes. Add the olives and garlic and sauté for another 2 minutes. Deglaze the pot with ¼ cup (60 mL) of the wine, scraping vigorously with a wooden spoon to help dissolve the solids that have formed. When the wine has reduced to a syrup, remove the liver to a platter and set aside, covered. Return all the other rabbit pieces to the pot, along with the juices from their platter. Add the remaining wine and bring to a boil. Reduce heat to a simmer and season lightly. When the wine has reduced by about half, add just enough stock to cover (you may not need all of it). Bring to a boil, then reduce heat to a bare simmer. Simmer, partially covered, for 30 minutes.

Remove the 2 forelegs to the platter with the liver. Continue to simmer, partially covered, for 20 minutes. Remove the saddle and rack to the platter. Continue to simmer until the hind legs are done, 15 minutes if boned or 25 minutes if the thigh bones were not removed. Return all the rabbit to the pot to heat through. Taste the sauce, adjust the seasonings, and sprinkle with parsley. Serve directly from the pot at the table.

Substitutions: Gaeta, Cerignolas, or any other top-quality olive—whether brined or salt-cured—can be used in place of the infornate olives. Beech, chanterelles, porcini, and other sought-after mushrooms can be substituted for the suggested combination. Chicken stock (page 286) may be used if rabbit stock is unavailable.

Variation: This basic but intensely flavoursome braise can be applied to a chicken almost as successfully as to a rabbit.

Side Dish Suggestions: Roast Potatoes with Rosemary and Garlic; Roasted Beets with Pistachios and Balsamic Vinegar; Spring Peas with Carrots and Rabbit Sauce

Suggested Wine: Roero Arneis or Chardonnay

Contorni

Side Dishes

Asparagi alla Griglia
Grilled Asparagus

Serves 6

2 large bunches green asparagus
2 tbsp (30 mL) olive oil
Salt and pepper
2 soft-poached eggs (optional)
2 oz (60 g) shaved Parmigiano-Reggiano
Fine olive oil
Cracked black pepper

Preheat grill on high.

Snap off the bottoms of the asparagus spears (they will break naturally at the point where they evolve from woody to tender). Blanch the asparagus for no more than 45 seconds in boiling salted water, and then shock them in ice water. Drain and pat dry. Toss in the olive oil, then season with salt and pepper and toss again. Grill the asparagus until lightly charred, about 1 minute per side. Arrange unidirectionally on a warm serving platter. If desired, top with the poached eggs. Then cover with the Parmesan, sprinkle generously with the fine olive oil, and finish with a scattering of cracked black pepper.

Piselli Novelli con Carote e Sugo di Coniglio
Spring Peas with Carrots and Rabbit Sauce

Serves 6

2 lb (1 kg) freshly shelled peas
1 lb (500 g) carrots, peeled
2 tbsp (30 mL) olive oil
Salt and pepper
2 cups (500 mL) rabbit stock (page 287)

Preheat oven to 450°F (230°C).

Lightly blanch the peas, shock in ice water, and drain. Blanch the carrots for 2 or 3 minutes, shock in ice water, and drain. Heat oil in a skillet, add the carrots, season, and transfer to the oven. Roast until thoroughly tender, about 8 minutes. Chop the carrots, then mash slightly with a fork. Combine the peas and carrots in a saucepan, add the stock, bring to a simmer, and simmer together for 3 minutes to heat through. Season to taste and serve.

Variation: Crispy pork enhances this mix: try adding ¼ cup (60 mL) of crumbled crisp pancetta—or crisply rendered diced bacon—along with the seasoning just before serving.

Substitution: You can use chicken stock (page 286) in place of the rabbit, but reduce it by half first, in order to simulate the viscosity of rabbit stock.

Bietole Saltate con Acciughe Bianche e Scorza di Limone Grattugiata
Sautéed Swiss Chard with White Anchovies and Lemon Zest

Serves 6

3 bunches Swiss chard
3 cloves garlic, minced
2 tbsp (30 mL) olive oil
½ cup (125 mL) white wine
Juice of 1 lemon
1 tbsp (15 mL) lemon zest
1 tbsp (15 mL) butter
Salt and pepper
12 oil-packed white anchovies (about 8 oz/250 g), drained

Trim the discoloured ends off the chard stalks. Then cut the stems from the leaves. Blanch the leaves in boiling, salted water until they wilt; transfer to a colander to drain. Blanch the stems separately until they soften, and then shock them in ice water.

In a very large skillet or sauté pan, sweat the garlic in the olive oil until it softens—but do not let it brown. Add the chard leaves and stems and raise the heat to medium-high. Sauté for 2 minutes, and then add the wine and lemon juice. Cook 2 minutes longer, then add the lemon zest and butter. Season with salt and pepper to taste. Transfer chard to a serving platter. Drape the anchovies over top.

Substitution: If you cannot locate lovely plump white anchovies, do not substitute the small, salty ones available by the tin at your local supermarket. They are not at all the same thing, and it's better to omit them altogether.

Radicchio Rosso di Treviso alla Griglia con Aceto Balsamico
Grilled Radicchio di Treviso with Balsamic Dressing

Serves 6

9 radicchio di Treviso
⅔ cup (150 mL) olive oil
⅓ cup (75 mL) balsamic vinegar
Salt and pepper

Preheat grill on high.

Halve the radicchio lengthwise and transfer to a baking dish. Whisk together the olive oil and balsamic vinegar; season to taste. Pour over the radicchio. Marinate on the countertop for 30 minutes, turning once or twice. Transfer the radicchio to the grill, reserving the marinade. Char it lightly on all sides. Transfer it to a warm platter. Whisk the marinade, and then pour ¼ cup (60 mL) over the radicchio. Season with salt and pepper, and serve.

Cavolo Nero Saltato con Speck
Sautéed Tuscan Black Kale with Speck

3 bunches black kale
4 oz (125 g) speck, diced
2 tbsp (30 mL) olive oil
3 tbsp (50 mL) basic soffritto (page 285)
Salt and pepper

Cut away and discard the stems from the kale. Blanch the leaves in boiling, salted water until they wilt, 8 to 10 minutes, and then drain in a colander. Meanwhile, in a large sauté pan, fry the speck in the olive oil over medium heat until it begins to crisp. Add the kale to the pan, and toss to mix with the speck and to heat through. Add the soffritto; toss and heat through. Season with salt and pepper to taste, and serve.

Substitutions: You may use other types of kale in place of the cavolo nero, and bacon in place of the speck.

Zucca in Agrodolce
Sweet-and-Sour Squash

Serves 6

1 butternut squash, about 10 inches (25 cm) long, halved, seeded, and peeled
⅓ cup (75 mL) olive oil
Salt and pepper
1 medium red onion, finely diced
1 cup (250 mL) red wine vinegar
½ tbsp (7 mL) balsamic vinegar
3 sprigs thyme
1 bay leaf
½ cup (125 mL) sugar

Preheat oven to 375°F (190°C).

Cut the squash into ½-inch (1 cm) cubes and spread on a baking sheet in a single layer. Sprinkle squash with about 3 tbsp (50 mL) of the olive oil, and season generously. Toss well to coat. Roast, turning with a spatula every 10 or 15 minutes, until tender and golden, about 45 minutes.

Meanwhile, in a sauté pan sweat the onion in the remaining 2 tbsp (30 mL) olive oil for 5 minutes. Add the red wine vinegar, balsamic vinegar, thyme, and bay leaf. Raise heat to bring to a boil, and then lower to a simmer. Cook, stirring occasionally, until the onion softens completely, about 5 more minutes. Stir in the sugar, and continue to simmer, stirring frequently, until it has completely dissolved.

Pour the onion over the squash and mix well. Taste and correct seasonings. Transfer the squash to a warm serving dish.

Substitutions: Any firm-fleshed sweet squash can be used in place of the butternut.

Carciofi Fritti
Deep-Fried Baby Artichokes

Serves 6

18 baby artichokes
Canola oil for deep-frying
1 batch *fritto misto* batter (see page 62)
Salt and pepper
1 lemon, cut into eighths
1 cup (250 mL) lemon-caper aïoli (optional; page 273)
Basil leaves (optional)

Trim the discoloured base of the stem, the tops, and the spiky points of the outer leaves from the artichokes. Cut them in half lengthwise and scrape out the choke if there is any. Blanch the artichoke halves in a large pot of boiling, salted water until just tender, between 2 and 4 minutes, depending on their size. Shock them in ice water.

Heat oil in a deep-fryer (or in a deep cast-iron skillet, filled to a depth of 1 inch/2.5 cm) to 360°F (180°C).

Drain the artichokes and shake dry. Dredge in the batter, and then deep-fry, turning if necessary, until golden and crisp all over. Remove to a bed of paper towels to drain briefly. Season generously, then arrange on a warm platter with lemon wedges. Garnish with basil leaves and serve with the optional aïoli on the side.

Barbabietole Arroste con Pistacchi
Roasted Beets with Pistachios

Serves 6

2 lb (1 kg) variegated beets, trimmed and scrubbed
3 tbsp (50 mL) olive oil
3 cloves garlic, thinly sliced
¼ bunch thyme
Salt and pepper
2 tbsp (30 mL) toasted pistachios, crushed
1 tbsp (15 mL) top-quality aged balsamic vinegar

Preheat oven to 400°F (200°C).

If the beets are of different sizes, halve or even quarter the larger ones so all the pieces are of roughly equal mass. Spread a sheet of foil on a work surface. Cluster the beets in a single layer at the centre. Drizzle with the olive oil. Scatter the garlic and thyme over top, and season well. Fold over the foil, seal it tightly, and wrap the package in a second sheet of foil. Roast for 45 minutes to an hour, depending on the size of the beets (squeeze them through the foil with a thick oven mitt to test for tenderness).

Allow the beets to cool for 10 minutes and then unwrap them. Transfer the beets with their juices to a warm serving dish. Sprinkle with the pistachios and finish with a drizzle of fine balsamic vinegar.

Substitution: If you do not have a genuinely exceptional balsamic on hand, enhance what you do have by turning it into a balsamic reduction (page 274).

Brasato di Finocchio con Pomodori e Sambuca
Braised Fennel with Tomato and Sambuca

Serves 6

3 medium fennel bulbs
3 tbsp (50 mL) olive oil
½ tbsp (7 mL) sugar
Salt and pepper
2 tbsp (30 mL) sambuca
3 tbsp (50 mL) white wine vinegar
1 tbsp (15 mL) toasted fennel seeds
1 can (28 oz/796 mL) San Marzano tomatoes, crushed
1½ cups (375 mL) *brodo* (page 3)
2 tbsp (30 mL) chopped oregano

Trim the stalks from the fennel bulbs. Halve each bulb lengthwise, and then cut each half into 3 wedges, leaving enough of the core intact to hold each wedge together. Transfer to a large bowl and toss with 1 tbsp (15 mL) of the olive oil, the sugar, and salt and pepper. Heat a large sauté pan on medium-high. Add the remaining 2 tbsp (30 mL) olive oil, and just before it smokes, carefully add the fennel wedges, jostling them with a wooden spoon so that they sit flat on their sides in maximum contact with the scorching-hot pan. When one side is bronzed, turn and repeat. When the second side is caramelized, add the sambuca and swirl it around the pan. When that has reduced to almost nothing, add the vinegar and fennel seeds. When the vinegar has reduced by half, add the tomatoes, *brodo*, and oregano. Bring to a boil, stir gently, lower the heat, and simmer, uncovered, until the fennel is tender, about 20 minutes. Taste and correct seasonings.

Cavolfiore Romanesco Gratinato
Roman Cauliflower with Cheese Sauce

Serves 6

1 batch *besciamella* (page 275)
4 oz (125 g) shredded provolone
3 oz (90 g) freshly shredded caciocavallo
2 oz (60 g) crumbled fresh goat cheese
2 oz (60 g) freshly grated Parmigiano-Reggiano
Salt and pepper
1 head Romanesca cauliflower, cored and cut into florets

Bring the *besciamella* to a simmer. Stir in the provolone, caciocavallo, goat cheese, and Parmesan, and fold gently until smooth. Taste, adjust seasonings, and keep warm. Blanch the cauliflower until just tender. Drain, and transfer to a serving dish. Pour over the hot cheese sauce and serve.

Substitutions: You may use regular cauliflower in place of the Romanesca, for a less colourful but similar result. Other, similar cheeses can be called upon to stand in for those listed above.

Patate Arroste con Rosmarino e Aglio
Roast Potatoes with Rosemary and Garlic

Serves 6

2½ tbsp (37 mL) olive oil
2 lb (1 kg) fingerling potatoes, scrubbed
1 tbsp (15 mL) butter
2 cloves garlic, minced
Leaves from 2 sprigs rosemary, chopped
Salt and cracked black pepper

Preheat oven to 375°F (190°C).

Lubricate a roasting pan just large enough to accommodate all the potatoes in a single layer with 2 tbsp (30 mL) of the olive oil. Halve the potatoes lengthwise. Arrange the potatoes in the pan cut side down without overlapping. Roast until tender and beginning to grow crisp and golden, about 45 minutes. Add the butter to the pan, swirl it around, and roast for 5 minutes longer.

Meanwhile, heat the remaining ½ tbsp (7 mL) olive oil in a small skillet and sweat the garlic until it softens—without browning it. Stir in the rosemary and turn off the heat. Transfer the potatoes to a warm serving bowl. Add the garlic-rosemary mixture, salt, and cracked pepper and toss well.

Dolci

Desserts

La Panna Cotta di Fabbrica
Vanilla Panna Cotta with Streusel and Figs

At its best, this Italian custard is silky, light, and refreshing—but at its worst, firm, dense, and excessively gelatinous. Ours aims for the former camp, using a minimum of gelatine to form a gently quivering custard. The streusel adds a welcome crunch, and the figs lend a requisite fruitiness. **Serves 4**

3 leaves gelatine
2 cups (500 mL) 35% cream
¼ cup (60 mL) sugar
½ vanilla bean

STREUSEL
½ cup (125 mL) cold butter
2 tbsp (30 mL) sugar
2 tbsp (30 mL) honey
¾ cup (175 mL) flour

SAUCE
¼ cup (60 mL) honey
¼ cup (60 mL) red port
½ sprig rosemary
½ vanilla bean
2 fresh figs, quartered

GARNISH
2 tbsp (30 mL) olive oil
½ vanilla bean
3 fresh figs, halved lengthwise
¼ cup (60 mL) sugar

SPECIAL EQUIPMENT
4 (4-inch/10 cm) ring moulds

Fold a 12-inch (30 cm) sheet of plastic wrap in half. Place a ring mould at its centre, lift the plastic wrap up around the edge, and secure it tautly in place with an elastic band to create a ramekin. Repeat with the remaining ring moulds. Arrange the ring moulds on a small baking sheet.

Submerge the gelatine in a bowl of ice-cold water. Place the cream and the sugar in a saucepan. Scrape the seeds from the vanilla bean into the cream, then add the pod. Gently bring to a simmer, stirring so the sugar dissolves. Discard the pod. Pour the mixture into a stainless steel bowl. Remove the gelatine leaves from the water, squeeze gently, and add them to the cream mixture. Whisk until dissolved. Place the bowl over a second, larger bowl of ice. Whisk gently until the cream mixture cools and thickens enough to coat the back of a spoon, about 10 minutes. Divide the mixture among the 4 ring moulds, cover with plastic wrap, and chill overnight.

Preheat oven to 325°F (160°C).

For the streusel, cut the butter into cubes and let it sit on the counter for 10 minutes. Transfer to the bowl of a stand mixer equipped with a paddle. Add the sugar and honey; mix on low speed. Once smooth, add the flour, mixing just until it attains a crumbly texture (do not mix further to form a dough). Scatter the crumble on a baking sheet, passing it through your fingers to break up any clumps. Bake, stirring now and then with a spatula, until golden and crisp, about 15 minutes.

For the sauce, combine the honey, port, and rosemary in a saucepan. Scrape the vanilla seeds into the pan and add the pod. Bring to a boil over medium-high heat. Reduce heat to a simmer and add the figs. Reduce the liquid by half. Strain through a sieve, pushing with a wooden spoon to force through the figs' seeds. Set aside at room temperature.

To finish, heat the oil in a skillet on medium heat. Add the vanilla bean. Dredge the cut side of the fig halves in the sugar, and then place them in the pan, once again cut side down. Cook until caramelized on that side, about 4 minutes. Remove from the pan, reserving the vanilla oil. Meanwhile, invert the moulds of panna cotta carefully onto 4 chilled plates. Remove the plastic wrap, pass the blade of a knife around the edge of the moulds, and then lift them away. Scatter a band of streusel across the top of the panna cotta. Halve the figs again, and place 3 segments on each plate. Drizzle lightly with the vanilla oil, follow with a spoonful of the port-fig sauce, and serve.

Tip: Whisking the panna cotta mixture as it cools suspends the flecks of vanilla in the cream as it coagulates. If you were to instead pour the warm mixture directly into the ring moulds, the vanilla seeds would sink to the bottom, leaving what will become the presentation side of the custard off-puttingly flecked with black specks.

Cannoli

There are those who consider Clemenza's memorable post-hit utterance in *The Godfather*—"Leave the gun. Take the cannoli"—one of those regrettable moments in popular culture that undermine the image of Italian Americans. But more enlightened types recognized it for great screenwriting—and as an incredible image boost for an already great dessert.

Makes 12 cannoli

4 tsp (20 mL) sugar
1 tbsp (15 mL) shortening
Pinch of salt
1 small egg
2 tsp (10 mL) white wine
2 tsp (10 mL) dry Marsala
¾ cup (175 mL) all-purpose flour, sifted

FILLING
½ cup (125 mL) buffalo ricotta, drained in cheesecloth for 24 hours
4 tsp (20 mL) fresh goat cheese
2 tbsp (30 mL) 2% milk
3 tbsp (50 mL) icing sugar
3 drops vanilla
Pinch of cinnamon
Pinch of grated lemon zest
½ cup (125 mL) mascarpone

TO FINISH
Canola oil for deep-frying
1 egg, lightly beaten
2 cups (500 mL) semi-sweet (52%) coating chocolate, warm (optional)
Icing sugar

SPECIAL EQUIPMENT
Metal cannoli rounds (about 5½ by ½ inch/13 by 1 cm)

Combine the sugar, shortening, and salt in a bowl. Work together with a rubber spatula until smooth. Add the egg and combine. Add half the white wine and half the Marsala, follow with half the flour, and mix thoroughly with the spatula. Repeat. Transfer the dough to a work surface and knead until smooth, about 5 minutes. Wrap the dough tightly in plastic wrap and transfer to the refrigerator to rest for at least 3 hours.

Meanwhile, for the filling, in a medium bowl combine the ricotta, goat cheese, and milk; work together with a rubber spatula until smooth. Add the icing sugar, vanilla, cinnamon, and lemon zest, and combine again. Finally, add the mascarpone, and whip with a whisk until the mixture forms peaks. Cover and refrigerate for at least 3 hours.

On a lightly floured surface, roll out the cannoli dough as thinly as possible, as if it were a sheet of pasta. Cut the dough into rectangles about 3 by 5 inches (8 by 13 cm). Stack the rectangles with small sheets of parchment paper in between them until needed (they can be refrigerated or even frozen this way).

Fill a cast-iron skillet to a depth of about ¾ inch (2 cm) with the canola oil and heat it to 375°F (190°C). Working with no more than 6 cannoli tubes at a time, lubricate the tubes with a little more canola oil. Wrap a rectangle of dough around each tube, brushing the inside edge of the overlap with the egg wash so that the dough stays firmly in place. Carefully transfer the tubes to the hot oil and fry, turning, until the shells are brown and crisp, about 45 seconds. Remove to a bed of paper towels to drain. When the tubes are cool, carefully slide off the cannoli. Repeat until you have 12 shells or all the dough is used.

To finish, if desired, dip one end of the shells in the coating chocolate, and then set aside on a parchment paper–lined baking sheet until set. Transfer the filling to a piping bag and pipe it into both ends of each cannoli until it is filled. Sprinkle the cannoli with icing sugar and serve.

Substitution: You may use a top-quality cow's milk ricotta in place of the buffalo variety.

Tip: If you have a pasta machine, do not hesitate to use it to roll out this dough—it works brilliantly.

Budino al Cioccolato con Noci Caramelizzate e Salsa di Mirtillo Rosso
Chocolate Cake with Caramel Nuts and Raspberry-Cranberry Sauce

This chocolate mousse cake strikes a perfect balance of rich chocolate flavour and a light, airy texture. Add to the equation the sauce and caramel nuts, and you have a chocolate dessert that is exquisitely close to perfect. Serves 6

SAUCE
½ cup (125 mL) dried cranberries
½ cup (125 mL) fresh or frozen raspberries
2 tbsp (30 mL) red port

TUILES (OPTIONAL)
2 tbsp (30 mL) butter
¼ cup (60 mL) icing sugar
1 egg white
¼ cup (60 mL) all-purpose flour

SALTED CARAMEL NUTS
1 cup (250 mL) sugar
½ cup (125 mL) corn syrup
1¼ cups (300 mL) 35% cream
¼ tsp (1 mL) pure vanilla extract
1 tsp (5 mL) grated milk chocolate
2 tbsp (30 mL) salted butter
⅓ cup (75 mL) mixed salted nuts (cashews,
    pine nuts, pistachios, pecans, peanuts, and the like)
1 egg white

BUDINO
4 eggs
8 oz (250 g) semisweet (52%) chocolate
½ cup (125 mL) butter
¼ cup (60 mL) sugar

GARNISH
1 batch salted caramel gelato (page 257; optional)
Icing sugar

SPECIAL EQUIPMENT
6 ring moulds (3 inches/8 cm wide and 2 inches/5 cm high)

For the sauce, combine the dried cranberries, raspberries, port, and ½ cup (125 mL) cold water in a saucepan. Bring to a boil and then simmer until the cranberries soften, about 7 minutes. Blitz in a blender (or with a hand blender). Pass through a sieve and reserve.

Preheat oven to 325°F (160°C). Line a baking sheet with a nonstick liner. Cut a 1½-by-½-inch (4 by 1 cm) rectangle from something no thicker than a shirt cardboard to use as a template.

For the tuiles, combine the butter and icing sugar in a bowl, and blend together well with a rubber spatula. Incorporate half the egg white, then half the flour; repeat. Using the cut-out template as a guide, spread the dough in thin strips on the lined baking sheet, as close together as your cut-out will allow. Bake until golden, about 7 minutes. While the tuiles are still hot, roll them gently in a spiral around the shaft of a wooden spoon, and then slide them off to set. (Do not turn the oven off.)

For the salted caramel nuts, combine the sugar and corn syrup in a saucepan on medium heat; cook, stirring frequently, until caramelized. Meanwhile, combine the cream and vanilla in a separate saucepan and bring to a boil. Slowly add the cream to the caramel, stirring all the while. Heat to 219°F (104°C). Pour into a bowl and let cool to 185°F (85°C). Whisk in the chocolate and then the butter, whisking until smooth. Spread the nuts on a baking sheet and brush them lightly with the egg white. Roast until golden, crisp, and fragrant, about 7 minutes. Let cool slightly, then transfer to a bowl. Fold in enough caramel to completely cover and bind them. Set aside.

Raise oven temperature to 350°F (180°C). Line a baking sheet with a nonstick liner. Cut parchment paper into six 10-by-3-inch (25 by 8 cm) strips and use them to line the ring moulds. Arrange the lined moulds on the baking sheet.

Place the eggs in a bowl of warm water. In a double boiler, melt together the chocolate and butter, stirring until smooth. Remove from the heat and set aside. Fill the bowl of a stand mixer with hot water and leave to sit for 5 minutes, then drain and dry. Crack in the eggs and whisk on high speed for 1 minute. Add the sugar and continue to whisk on high speed until the mixture forms high, stiff peaks. Add one-third of the egg mixture to the chocolate mixture and fold together until just mixed (it should be streaky). Add this mixture back to the egg mixture. Using a rubber spatula, gently but thoroughly combine the two, aerating the mixture by lifting it from the centre outward rather than pushing it down the sides of the bowl. When the mixture is well combined, transfer it to a large measuring cup. Pour the cake mixture into the ring moulds to a height of about 2 inches (5 cm). Cover the moulds with a sheet of parchment paper, and then weight it down with a second nonstick liner. Bake for 15 minutes, rotate the tray, and bake for another 15 minutes. The budino should be pulling away from the edge of the ring moulds, and the surface should be mildly tacky to the touch. Set aside to cool slightly.

To finish, arrange an artful smear of the sauce on each of 6 plates. Gently place a *budino* alongside and then lift off the mould. Divide the nuts among the plates, making small mounds on the plate or the cake, and place a small scoop of gelato directly on top (optional). Decorate with a tuile, if desired, then sprinkle each *budino* with icing sugar and serve.

Tip: Only about ½ cup (125 mL) of the caramel is required. The rest can be stored in the refrigerator for up to 6 months.

Gelato
Italian Ice Cream

The fundamental difference between gelato and other ice cream is that the former contains less milk fat—less cream, more milk. This may come as a surprise to some gelato enthusiasts, because gelato so often tastes richer than its more commonplace counterpart. That brings us to their second primary difference: as gelato is usually mixed at a slower speed, it ultimately has less air in its mix, and so achieves richness through density. Okay, all those egg yolks help, too—but it remains a neat trick, and one that is easy and rewarding to duplicate at home. **Makes about 6 cups (1.5 L)**

Apricot Gelato

2 cups (500 mL) whole milk
1 cup (250 mL) 35% cream
10 egg yolks

⅔ cup (150 mL) sugar
1½ lb (750 g) ripe apricots, peeled, pitted, and chopped

Combine the milk and cream in a saucepan, and scald on high heat. In a bowl, whisk together the egg yolks and sugar until thick and pale. Temper the egg mixture—so that it will not curdle—by vigorously whisking in ¼ cup (60 mL) of the hot milk mixture. Slowly add the rest of the hot milk mixture, whisking all the while. Stir in the apricots. Transfer the mixture to a clean saucepan and—stirring constantly and making sure the spoon reaches the bottom of the pot—slowly bring it to a temperature of 185°F (85°C). Pour the mixture into a bowl placed inside another, larger bowl half full of ice water, and whisk vigorously to chill it. Cover the mixture and transfer it to the refrigerator to chill thoroughly. Transfer to an ice-cream maker and follow the manufacturer's instructions.

Pistachio Gelato

4 oz (125 g) pistachios, toasted, shelled, and chopped

Follow the recipe for apricot gelato, but replace the apricots with the pistachios.

Salted Caramel Gelato

¾ cup (175 mL) sugar
2 tbsp (30 mL) butter
½ tsp (2 mL) fleur de sel

Combine the sugar and 1 tbsp (15 mL) cold water in a small saucepan. Heat over medium heat, stirring constantly, until caramelized. Allow to cool slightly, then stir in the butter and fleur de sel. Follow the recipe for apricot gelato (omitting the apricots), adding the scalded milk first to the caramel and stirring until mixed before adding to the egg mixture.

Il Tiramisù di Fabbrica
Tiramisù

This simple dessert is an indisputable classic of new Italian cuisine. Our take forgoes the standard coffee-sodden ladyfingers in favour a freshly made, coffee-brushed white chocolate sponge cake. The result is more luxurious, and a lot less mushy. **Serves 8 to 10**

CHOCOLATE CARAMEL CRUNCH
⅔ cup (150 mL) sugar
2 tbsp (30 mL) corn syrup
2 tbsp (30 mL) butter
1 oz (30 g) dark chocolate, chopped

FRAPPUCCINO (OPTIONAL)
1 can (300 mL) condensed milk
2 long espressos

SPONGE CAKE
4 eggs
1 cup (250 mL) all-purpose flour
1 oz (30 g) Chocolate Caramel Crunch (optional)
½ cup (125 mL) sugar
4 oz (125 g) white chocolate, chopped

MASCARPONE CREAM
1 leaf gelatine
1 short espresso
½ cup (125 mL) icing sugar
10 oz (300 g) mascarpone
⅔ cup (150 mL) 35% cream, whipped

COFFEE SYRUP
¼ cup (60 mL) sugar
1 long espresso

GARNISH
Cocoa powder
Whipped cream (optional)

For the crunch, spread a large sheet of parchment paper on a work surface. Combine the sugar, corn syrup, and ¼ cup (60 mL) cold water in a saucepan. Cook, stirring frequently, over medium-low heat until golden and thoroughly caramelized. Remove from the heat, stir in the butter, and follow with the chocolate, stirring until melted and smooth. Drop the caramel 1 tsp (5 mL) at a time onto the parchment paper, immediately spreading it with a small offset spatula into a long, thin smear. Your goal is for semi-translucent strips of hardened caramel about 1 inch (2 cm) wide and 4 inches (10 cm) long. If the caramel in the saucepan becomes too thick to work with, gently reheat it. When the sheets are done, set aside in a cool place.

If you intend to make the frappuccino, place the can of condensed milk in a small, deep saucepan, cover it completely with water, and simmer on low heat for 3 hours, topping up the water to keep the can covered as required.

For the sponge cake, preheat oven to 350°F (180°C). Butter a 10-inch (25 cm) springform pan.

Place the eggs in a bowl of warm water and set aside for 5 minutes. Meanwhile, sift the flour into a small bowl, crumble the caramel crunch into it, and mix well. Crack the eggs into the bowl of a stand mixer and whisk on high speed until blended and beginning to froth. Add the sugar, and continue whisking until the volume has more than doubled and the mixture forms stiff peaks, about 7 minutes. Melt the chocolate in a double-boiler, stirring until smooth. With the mixer on low speed, add the melted chocolate. Turn off the mixer and use a rubber spatula to scrape the bottom of the bowl and ensure that everything is properly incorporated. With the mixer on low speed, add half the flour mixture, and mix until it is incorporated. Add the remaining flour mixture and fold it in with the spatula. Pour the mixture into the springform pan. Bake until the cake is golden and a skewer inserted into the centre emerges clean, about 20 minutes. Cool the cake on a rack, and then transfer to the refrigerator to chill.

For the mascarpone cream, submerge the gelatine in a bowl of cold water. Combine the espresso and icing sugar in a small saucepan. Stir over low heat until the sugar is dissolved. Squeeze the gelatine, add it to the saucepan, and stir again until dissolved. Transfer to a small bowl, and whisk in a scoop of the mascarpone. Transfer the remaining mascarpone to a large bowl, add the tempered espresso mixture, and whisk together until combined. Follow with the whipped cream, and whisk again. Transfer to the refrigerator to chill and thicken.

For the coffee syrup, combine the sugar with ¼ cup (60 mL) cold water in a small saucepan and stir over low heat until the sugar is just dissolved. Set aside to cool. Stir in the espresso, transfer to a shallow bowl, and chill in the refrigerator.

To finish the frappuccino, whisk together half the simmered condensed milk with the 2 long espressos; refrigerate until cool.

To finish, cut the cake into 8 to 10 wedges. Dip each wedge into the chilled coffee syrup, flipping it in the liquid swiftly to cover. Arrange each dipped slice on a plate. Transfer the mascarpone cream to a piping bag and pipe a layer on top of each piece of cake. Follow with a sheet of caramel crunch, then a second layer of cream, and a final sheet of caramel crunch. If you made the frappuccino, shake it with crushed ice and serve in a small glass on the plate, topped with whipped cream. Sprinkle cocoa over the cake and the frappuccino and serve at once.

Tip: For best results, avoid even remotely granular mascarpone for this recipe and use the finest, smoothest Italian variety (like Foresti).

Shortcuts: While they make enjoyable additions to the finished plate, neither the caramel crunch nor the frappuccino is at all essential to this tiramisù. As well, the white chocolate sponge cake will still turn out admirably without any crumbled caramel in its batter. So feel free to save time by omitting both these elements, and simply serve the dipped cake topped with mascarpone-coffee cream.

Budino di Riso
Rice Pudding

There is probably no other dessert as internationally ubiquitous as rice pudding—it is entrenched across Asia, Europe, and the Americas alike. This is perhaps in some large part because its principal ingredients are such fundamental staples—rice and milk. The ease of its preparation helps too. But above all else, it tastes awfully good, especially when you make it with arborio rice, as we do at Fabbrica. **Serves 6**

¾ cup (175 mL) arborio rice
5 cups (1.25 L) whole milk
½ vanilla bean
½ cup (125 mL) sugar
3 tbsp (50 mL) butter

Combine the rice and milk in a saucepan. Scrape the seeds from the vanilla bean and add the seeds to the pot. Bring to a boil over medium heat, stir, and lower the heat to a simmer. Cook, uncovered and stirring frequently, until the rice is just tender, about 40 minutes. Stir in the sugar and continue simmering until the rice is very tender, another 10 minutes. Stir in the butter until melted, cover, and set aside for 10 minutes. Serve warm.

Zeppole
Doughnuts with Pastry Cream Filling and White Chocolate Dipping Sauce

Nearly all cuisines of note feature a version of what North Americans call the doughnut. The Italian take, *zeppole*, typically features a custard or pastry cream filling—which in our version is brightened with orange zest. Then we up the ante with a dipping sauce of white chocolate ganache. **Makes 20 to 30 *zeppole***

DOUGH
½ cup (125 mL) warm 2% milk
1 package (8 g) active dry yeast (or ½ ounce/14 g fresh yeast)
1 egg
1¾ cups (425 mL) all-purpose flour, sifted
2 tbsp (30 mL) butter, softened
2 tbsp (30 mL) sugar
Canola oil for deep-frying

PASTRY CREAM FILLING
½ cup (125 mL) 2% milk
⅓ cup (75 mL) 35% cream
½ tsp (2 mL) grated orange zest
1 egg
2 tbsp (30 mL) sugar
1 tbsp (15 mL) cornstarch

DIPPING SAUCE
¾ cup (175 mL) 35% cream
½ vanilla bean
½ tsp (2 mL) grated orange zest
4 oz (125 g) white chocolate, chopped
2 tbsp (30 mL) thick plain yogurt

GARNISH
Granulated sugar seasoned with cinnamon

If using fresh yeast, combine in a bowl with the warm milk, half the flour, and a pinch of sugar; whisk thoroughly. Sprinkle with a little flour and set aside in a warm place to rise for 30 minutes. Transfer to the bowl of a stand mixer equipped with a dough hook, add the rest of the flour, the egg, butter, and sugar, and blend on low speed until the ingredients combine in a ball of dough. (If using instant yeast, simply combine the milk, yeast, egg, flour, butter, and sugar in the bowl of the stand mixer and blend on low speed until the ingredients come together in a ball of dough.) The dough should be soft and tacky. If it seems excessively damp, add a little more flour and mix again. Transfer the dough to a work surface and knead for about 1 minute. Transfer to a lightly floured bowl, sprinkle with flour, cover, and allow to rise for 30 minutes. Punch down, cover, and refrigerate overnight.

For the filling, combine the milk, cream, and orange zest in a saucepan. Bring to a gentle boil over medium heat, then set aside. In a small bowl, whisk together the egg, sugar, and cornstarch. Add about ¼ cup (60 mL) of the hot cream mixture to the egg mixture, and whisk vigorously. Then add the tempered egg mixture to the cream mixture, whisk again, and return to medium heat. Stir constantly until the mixture bubbles and thickens, then transfer to a clean bowl and cover with plastic wrap, pressing it onto the surface. Leave it to cool on the counter for about 10 minutes, then transfer to the refrigerator until thoroughly chilled, about 1 hour.

Meanwhile, for the sauce, pour the cream into a small saucepan. Scrape the vanilla seeds from the pod, then add the seeds, pod, and the orange zest to the cream. Bring to a gentle boil over medium heat. Discard the vanilla pod. Pour the cream over the chocolate in a bowl, and whisk until the chocolate is melted and smooth. Set aside to cool on the counter for about 10 minutes, then transfer to the refrigerator until thoroughly chilled, about 1 hour.

Line a baking sheet with parchment paper and sprinkle lightly with flour. Punch down the chilled dough. Roll it into balls about 1 inch (2.5 cm) in diameter and transfer to the baking sheet. Set aside to proof for 1 hour.

Meanwhile, heat oil in a deep-fryer (or in a deep cast-iron skillet) to 375°F (180°C). Whisk the yogurt into the chilled white chocolate sauce. Whisk the chilled pastry cream filling and transfer to a piping bag fitted with its pointiest tip. Working in batches, gently add *zeppole* to the hot oil, rotating a few times on the surface until they begin to crisp, and then placing the deep-fryer basket (or, if you are using a skillet, a wire skimmer) on top of them to submerge them until completely bronzed, about 2 minutes. With a slotted spoon remove *zeppole* to drain very briefly on paper towels, then roll them in the cinnamon sugar. While they are still warm, pierce them with the tip of the piping bag and fill them with pastry cream. Serve *zeppole* with a bowl of white chocolate sauce for dipping.

Torta di Ricotta e Limone
Ricotta and Meyer Lemon Cheesecake

Everybody loves cheesecake. Yet this one—with a buffalo ricotta–based filling lightened with lemon zest—will make even an experienced enthusiast reconsider what came before.

Makes 1 cheesecake

CRUST
3½ cups (875 mL) Rice Krispies
½ cup (125 mL) loosely packed brown sugar
½ cup (125 mL) butter, melted
Grated zest of 1 Meyer lemon or ½ lemon

FILLING
7 oz (200 g) ricotta di bufala, drained in cheesecloth for 24 hours, at room temperature
7 oz (200 g) cream cheese, at room temperature
⅓ cup (75 mL) sour cream
⅓ cup (75 mL) sugar
1 tbsp (15 mL) cornstarch
1 tsp (5 mL) grated lemon zest (preferably Meyer)
2 eggs, at room temperature
2 oz (60 g) white chocolate, chopped
2 tbsp (30 mL) 35% cream
¼ cup (60 mL) Meyer lemon juice

GLAZE
¼ cup (60 mL) sugar
3 tbsp (50 mL) Meyer lemon juice
12 Meyer lemon segments, membranes removed
2 strips lemon zest, blanched and minced
4 tsp (20 mL) limoncello

PRESERVED BLUEBERRIES (OPTIONAL)
2 pints (1 L) fresh blueberries, picked over
2 tbsp (30 mL) sugar
Juice of ½ lemon

Preheat oven to 300°F (150°C). Butter a 10-inch (30 cm) springform pan.

For the crust, thoroughly crush the Rice Krispies with your hands or in a food processor until they have the texture of coarse bread crumbs. Stir in the brown sugar, butter, and lemon zest until thoroughly combined. Press the mixture into the base of the pan until it compresses into a crust. (You may use less if you prefer a thinner crust.) Chill for 1 hour.

Meanwhile, make the filling. Combine the ricotta and cream cheese in the bowl of a stand mixer fitted with the paddle, and mix at low speed for 2 minutes. Add the sour cream and mix until incorporated. Stop the mixer and scrape the base of the bowl with a rubber spatula to ensure no ingredients remain stuck there and unincorporated. In a small bowl, combine the sugar, cornstarch, and zest. With the mixer on low speed, add the dry ingredients just until blended. Add the eggs 1 at a time, mixing well after each addition. Meanwhile, heat the chocolate and cream over a double boiler, and whisk together until combined. Whisk in the lemon juice. Add the chocolate mixture to the ricotta mixture and mix until smooth and uniform. Once again, stop the mixer and scrape the bottom of the mixing bowl. Mix a final time.

Pour the filling into the springform pan. Bake for 30 minutes. Rotate the pan and bake for 15 minutes more. The filling should appear firm and not jiggle excessively when moved about. Cool on a rack for 30 minutes, and then transfer to the refrigerator until thoroughly chilled, about 3 hours.

Meanwhile, for the glaze, combine the sugar and 1 tbsp (15 mL) cold water in a small saucepan over medium heat. Cook, stirring occasionally, until lightly caramelized. Stir in the lemon juice, lemon segments, and lemon zest. Cook, stirring frequently, until reduced by half. Allow the mixture to cool slightly, then add the limoncello. Blitz in a blender (or with a hand blender). Transfer to a small container and refrigerate until cool and thickened, about 1 hour. Brush over the chilled cheesecake before or after the mould is removed.

If you wish to include the preserved blueberries, transfer the berries to a saucepan and cook on medium-low heat until thoroughly softened. Add the sugar and stir until dissolved. Stir in the lemon juice and reduce to desired consistency. Chill. Pour 1 tbsp (15 mL) over each serving of glazed cheesecake.

Substitutions: If you cannot find buffalo ricotta you may use a top-quality cow's milk variety. Meyer lemons are sweeter and less acidic, but regular lemons will do in their place.

Basic Recipes

Aïoli

Basic (Lemon-Garlic)

Makes 1¹/₂ cups (375 mL)

1 egg
1 clove garlic, minced
1 cup (250 mL) vegetable oil
2 tbsp (30 mL) lemon juice
Salt and pepper

Whisk together the egg and garlic. While continuing to whisk, begin adding the oil in a steady trickle. When all the oil has been incorporated and the mixture is emulsified, whisk in the lemon juice to thin. Then season. The aïoli keeps, refrigerated, for 3 days.

Carpaccio Aïoli

Make the basic aïoli. Add 1 tbsp (15 mL) each Dijon and grainy mustard. Whisk, and finish with another 2 tbsp (30 mL) lemon juice.

Crab Aïoli

Make the basic aïoli. Add 2 tbsp (30 mL) crab reduction, 2 tbsp (30 mL) chopped parsley, and ½ tsp (2 mL) cracked black pepper. Whisk, and finish with another 2 tbsp (30 mL) lemon juice.

Cured Tomato Aïoli

Make the basic aïoli. Transfer to a food processor. Chop 8 pieces of cured (or sun-dried) tomato, add to the bowl, and pulse.

Lemon-Caper Aïoli

Make the basic aïoli. Add 3 tbsp (50 mL) of (preferably salt-packed) capers, rinsed, drained, and chopped. Whisk, and finish with another 2 tbsp (30 mL) lemon juice.

Antipasto Spread

Makes about 2¹/₂ cups (625 mL)

2 tbsp (30 mL) olive oil
½ cup (125 mL) cauliflower florets
1 clove garlic, sliced
¼ cup (60 mL) red wine
1 cup (250 mL) ketchup
½ cup (125 mL) chopped cured (oven-dried or sun-dried) tomatoes
1 tsp (5 mL) minced oregano
½ cup (125 mL) diced grilled Sicilian eggplant
¼ cup (60 mL) julienned peeled roasted red pepper
¼ cup (60 mL) julienned green pepper
½ small carrot, julienned
4 cremini mushrooms, sliced
¼ cup (60 mL) chopped green olives
2 tbsp (30 mL) chopped black olives
4 anchovy fillets, chopped
1 tbsp (15 mL) chopped sour gherkin
¼ tsp (1 mL) minced preserved chili
Salt and pepper

In a skillet or sauté pan, sauté the cauliflower in 1 tbsp (15 mL) of the olive oil until lightly browned; remove with a slotted spoon. Add the remaining olive oil and the garlic to the pan, and sauté until the garlic is softened but not browned, about 1 minute. Deglaze with the red wine. When that has reduced to a syrup, stir in the ketchup, preserved tomato, and oregano. Cook for 2 minutes. Add the eggplant, red and green peppers, carrot, mushrooms, green and black olives, anchovies, gherkins, chili, and the reserved cauliflower. Stir, bring to a boil, and then lower heat and simmer for 10 minutes. Pulse in a food processor until well combined but still textured—not smooth. Taste and adjust seasonings.

Balsamic Reduction

Makes ¹/₂ cup (125 mL)

1 cup (250 mL) ordinary balsamic vinegar
¼ cup (60 mL) sugar

Bring the vinegar and sugar to a simmer, stirring to dissolve the sugar, and reduce by a third to a half over low heat.

Besciamella

Makes 2 cups (500 mL)

2 cup (250 mL) milk
1 yellow onion
1 bay leaf
1 clove
3 tbsp (30 mL) butter
3 tbsp (30 mL) all-purpose flour
Salt and pepper

Bring the milk to a simmer in a saucepan. Meanwhile, peel and trim the onion, and pin the bay leaf to one of its ends with the clove. Place the saucepan on a simmering plate at the lowest possible temperature, add the onion to the hot milk, and let steep for 15 minutes. Meanwhile, in a separate saucepan, melt the butter over medium-low heat, and as the foam subsides, add the flour. Cook, stirring, for 2 minutes (do not brown the flour). Discard the onion, and then slowly add the milk to the roux, whisking the whole while. Continue cooking until the sauce is thick and smooth, about 10 minutes. Adjust seasoning.

Bone Marrow Butter

Makes about 1 cup (250 mL)

4 beef marrow bones (each about 6 inches/18 cm and 4 lb/2 kg total), split lengthwise
½ cup (125 mL) cold butter, cubed
Salt and pepper

Place the marrow bones in a large pot, fill it with cold water, and refrigerate overnight, changing the water several times. Preheat oven to 450°F (230°C). Drain the bones, pat them dry, and arrange them marrow side up in a roasting pan. Roast until bronzed and the marrow yields easily when pierced with a fork, about 20 minutes. Set aside to rest. Remove the butter from the refrigerator and leave to warm on the countertop for about 10 minutes. Scrape the warm marrow from the bones into a bowl and add the cool butter. Mix well with a rubber spatula to form a paste. Pass through a fine sieve into a clean bowl and season to taste.

Bone Marrow Focaccia Croutons

Makes about 2 cups (500 mL)

½ loaf focaccia
½ cup (125 mL) bone marrow butter (page 275)

Gently melt the marrow butter over low heat. Tear crouton-sized morsels of focaccia crumb from between the crusts until you have about 2 cups (500 mL). Toss in the melted marrow butter until infused. Fry the croutons over medium-low heat until golden and crisp. Allow to cool before using.

Caponata

½ cup (125 mL) olive oil
1 medium eggplant, diced, salted, drained for 2 hours
1 medium onion, diced
2 stalks celery, diced
½ fennel bulb, diced
1 small zucchini, diced
3 Roma tomatoes, cored and diced
Leaves from ½ bunch basil
⅓ cup (75 mL) red wine vinegar
3 tbsp (50 mL) toasted pine nuts
3 tbsp (50 mL) raisins
1 tbsp (15 mL) tomato paste
Pinch of sugar
Salt and pepper

Heat 2 tbsp (30 mL) of the olive oil in a skillet on medium-high, and sauté the eggplant until lightly browned and softened. Transfer to a saucepan with a slotted spoon. Add 3 tbsp (45 mL) olive oil to the skillet, and follow with the onion, celery, fennel, zucchini, and tomatoes. Cook, stirring frequently, until the vegetables are just beginning to soften, then add to the eggplant. Stir in the remaining olive oil, basil, vinegar, pine nuts, raisins, tomato paste, sugar, and salt and pepper, and bring to a simmer for 3 minutes. Remove from the heat, cover, and let steep for 2 hours. (The caponata tastes best after 2 days in the refrigerator.)

Crisp Pancetta

Preheat oven to 325°F (160°C). Place thin slices of pancetta on a baking sheet lined with parchment paper and bake until crisp, about 15 minutes.

Crispy-Fried Capers

1 cup (250 mL) canola oil
¼ cup (60 mL) rinsed and drained capers

In a small skillet, heat the oil until it is nearly smoking. Pat the capers dry with a paper towel, and—standing well back—add them to the hot oil. As they puff up and crisp in the heat, remove them with a slotted spoon and drain on paper towels.

Crispy-Fried Sage or Parsley

1 cup (250 mL) vegetable or olive oil
Sage or parsley leaves

In a small skillet, heat the oil until it is nearly smoking. Drop the leaves right in, 1 small batch at a time. When they darken and shrivel, remove with a slotted spoon and drain on paper towels.

Horseradish Gremolata

½ cup (125 mL) bone marrow focaccia croutons (page 276) or other buttery croutons, crushed
Grated zest of 2 lemons
¼ cup (60 mL) chopped parsley
½ tsp (2 mL) minced oregano
1 tbsp (15 mL) grated Parmigiano-Reggiano
Salt and pepper
1-inch (2.5 cm) piece peeled horseradish

In a bowl, combine the bread crumbs, zest, parsley, and oregano; mix well. Add the cheese, season lightly, and mix again. Grate half the horseradish into the bowl, toss, and taste. Add more horseradish if desired. Correct seasonings and use at once. (If you wish to make the gremolata ahead of time, combine only the bread crumbs, zest, and herbs; keep refrigerated in a sealed container. Add cheese and horseradish just before use.)

Lamb Sausage
Makes 20 small links

½ lb (250 g) fatty lamb (such as shoulder), cubed
1½ lb (750 g) lean lamb (such as leg), cubed
1 tbsp (15 mL) combined minced rosemary, thyme, oregano, and arugula
1 tbsp (15 mL) kosher salt
¾ tsp (4 mL) black pepper
¾ tsp (4 mL) toasted fennel seeds, ground
½ tsp (2 mL) white pepper
½ tsp (2 mL) garlic powder
1 tsp (5 mL) brown sugar
Pork or lamb sausage casing, rinsed

Pass the fatty lamb through a meat grinder equipped with a medium blade. Combine the mince with the cubed lean lamb, then pass them together through the meat grinder into a large bowl. Add the herbs, salt, black pepper, fennel seeds, white pepper, and garlic powder. Mix thoroughly by hand, lifting the mixture from the bowl and squeezing it between your fingers. Dissolve the brown sugar in ½ cup (125 mL) ice-cold water, and then incorporate it into the meat mixture. Remove a small sample, sear it, taste, and adjust seasonings. Transfer the sausage meat into the funnel of a sausage maker, compressing it as much as possible to eliminate air pockets. Feed the filling into the sausage casing, tying off small links 3 inches (7.5 cm) as you go. Rest sausages in the refrigerator for at least 30 minutes before using.

Peperonata

3 tbsp (50 mL) olive oil
2 medium onions, sliced
2 red bell peppers, sliced
2 yellow bell peppers, sliced
1 clove garlic, thinly sliced
1 sprig rosemary
1 tbsp (15 mL) balsamic vinegar
Salt and pepper

Heat the olive oil in a sauté pan on medium heat. Add the onions, red and yellow peppers, garlic, and rosemary. Stir for 2 minutes, then lower heat to lowest setting. Simmer gently, stirring occasionally, for 1 hour. Stir in the balsamic vinegar, season, and set aside to steep for at least an hour before serving. (The peperonata tastes best after being refrigerated overnight.)

Pestos

Basil

Makes about ¹/₂ cup (125 mL)

Leaves from 1 bunch basil
¼ cup (60 mL) olive oil
3 tbsp (50 mL) toasted pine nuts
1 clove garlic, minced
4 tsp (20 mL) freshly grated Parmigiano-Reggiano
Salt and pepper
Squeeze of lemon juice

Combine the basil, olive oil, pine nuts, and garlic in a food processor, and pulse until smooth. Add the cheese, salt, pepper, and lemon juice; pulse again. Taste, correct seasonings, and add more lemon juice if desired.

Oregano

Makes about ³/₄ cup (175 mL)

1 cup (250 mL) lightly packed oregano leaves
½ cup (125 mL) lightly packed parsley leaves
½ cup (125 mL) olive oil
Juice of 1 lemon
1 clove garlic, minced
Salt and pepper

Combine the oregano, parsley, olive oil, lemon juice, garlic, and salt and pepper in a food processor, and pulse until smooth. Taste and correct seasonings.

Potato Gnocchi

Makes 4 main-course servings

5 medium Yukon Gold potatoes (about 2 lb/1 kg), scrubbed
1 tbsp (15 mL) salt
Pinch each of white pepper and nutmeg
1 tbsp (15 mL) clarified butter
¼ cup (60 mL) grated Parmigiano-Reggiano
1 small clove garlic, minced
1 egg, lightly beaten
½ cup plus 1 tbsp (140 mL) all-purpose flour

Preheat oven to 375°F (190°C). Roast the potatoes until cooked through, 50 to 60 minutes. Cut them open halfway, squeeze to open slightly, and return them to the oven for a further 10 minutes to drive out steam. Let cool briefly, then scoop out the flesh and pass it through a ricer into a bowl. Add the salt, pepper, nutmeg, butter, Parmesan, garlic, and egg. Mix well, lifting the mixture and then letting it fall through your fingers so that it is aerated by the process rather than compressed. Add a third of the flour and mix again in the same manner. Repeat until all the flour is incorporated. Press the mixture together lightly. It should be just barely tacky to the touch. If it is sticky, incorporate a little more flour. Set dough aside to rest for a few minutes.

Flour a work surface. Working in batches, roll the dough into a log about ¾ inch (2 cm) in diameter. Flour a knife, trim the end of the log at an angle, and—maintaining that angle—cut the log into roughly 1-inch (2.5 cm) pieces. Transfer gnocchi to a lightly floured baking sheet.

Roasted Garlic Peppers

Makes about 2 cups (500 mL)

3 red bell peppers
3 yellow bell peppers
10 cloves garlic, sliced
¼ cup (60 mL) chopped parsley
2 tbsp (30 mL) chopped rosemary
1 tbsp (15 mL) minced oil-preserved red chilies
Salt and pepper
2 cups (500 mL) olive oil

Char, peel, and julienne the peppers. Combine in a bowl with the garlic, parsley, rosemary, and chilies. Season, and toss well. Add just enough olive oil to cover. Leave to marinate on the countertop for 1 hour. If not using right away, transfer to a sealable container and store in the refrigerator.

Soffrittos

Basic

½ cup (125 mL) olive oil
2 cups (500 mL) minced onion
1 cup (250 mL) minced fennel
1 cup (250 mL) minced celery
1 cup (250 mL) minced carrot

Heat the oil in a sauté pan on medium-high. Add all the vegetables and stir frequently to prevent their acquiring any colour. After 5 minutes lower heat to lowest setting. Continue cooking until vegetables are completely soft, about 1 hour.

Blond

Substitute an equal quantity of minced white part of leek for the carrot.

Stocks, *Jus*, Essences, and Reductions

Crab or Shrimp Stock

Makes about 2 quarts (2 L)

3 lb (1.5 kg) crab or shrimp shells, rinsed
2 tbsp (30 mL) olive oil
½ cup (125 mL) white wine
½ Spanish onion, sliced
1 leek (white part only), sliced
1 stalk celery, sliced
1 lemon, halved
¼ bunch parsley
3 bay leaves
10 black peppercorns

Sauté the shells in the olive oil over high heat for 3 minutes. Deglaze with the wine. When that has nearly evaporated, add all the other ingredients, along with 2½ quarts (2.5 L) cold water. Bring to a boil, reduce heat to a simmer, and skim the scum from the surface. Simmer, uncovered, for 2 hours, continuing to skim scum as it rises. Strain the stock. Stock keeps 3 days in the fridge or 6 months in the freezer.

Crab Essence

Reduce strained crab stock by three-quarters.

Crab Reduction

Reduce crab essence by half.

Fish Stock

Makes about 2 quarts (2 L)

2 lb (1 kg) white fish bones (such as halibut, sole, turbot, flounder), rinsed and chopped
½ Spanish onion, sliced
1 small leek (white part only), sliced
16 stems parsley without leaves

3 bay leaves
12 peppercorns
1 lemon, sliced
1 cup (250 mL) white wine
2 tbsp (30 mL) kosher salt

Combine all the ingredients in a heavy, nonreactive stock pot. Add 2 quarts (2 L) cold water, bring to a boil, reduce heat, and simmer for an hour or so, skimming scum from the surface as it rises. Strain. Keeps for about 3 days in the fridge and about 6 months in the freezer.

Pork, Veal, or White Chicken Stock

Makes about 12 quarts (12 L)

10 lb (4.5 kg) pork, veal, or chicken bones, cut into pieces and well rinsed
3 medium Spanish onions, very coarsely chopped
2 large carrots, very coarsely chopped

½ bunch celery, very coarsely chopped
½ bunch thyme
¼ bunch parsley
4 bay leaves
1 tbsp (15 mL) black peppercorns

In a stock pot, cover the bones with about 15 quarts (15 L) cold water. Bring to a boil, reduce heat to a simmer, and skim the scum from the surface. When the scum subsides, add the remaining ingredients. Simmer, uncovered, for at least 3 hours, continuing to skim the scum as it rises and replenishing the water as needed. Strain stock, chill, and skim fat from the surface. Keeps for about 1 week in the fridge and about 6 months in the freezer.

Note: Stock is an invaluable commodity for keeping on hand in the freezer. If the quantity above is too much for your needs, use the reduced quantities outlined in the Rabbit Stock recipe.

Rabbit Stock

Makes about 3 quarts (3 L)

3 lb (1.5 kg) rabbit bones, chopped and rinsed
1 medium Spanish onion, very coarsely chopped
1 medium carrot, very coarsely chopped
3 stalks celery, very coarsely chopped
3 sprigs thyme
3 sprigs parsley
2 bay leaves
1 tsp (5 mL) black peppercorns

In a Dutch oven, cover the bones with about 4 quarts (4 L) cold water. Follow directions for Beef, Veal, or White Chicken Stock on page 286.

Veal *Jus*

Makes about 5 cups (1.25 L)

10 lb (4.5 kg) veal bones, cut into pieces and well rinsed
3 medium Spanish onions, very coarsely chopped
2 medium carrots, very coarsely chopped
½ bunch celery, very coarsely chopped
¼ bunch parsley
1 sprig rosemary
1 sprig sage
3 Roma tomatoes, halved
3 cups (750 mL) red wine
10 quarts (10 L) veal stock

Preheat oven to 450°F (230°C). Roast the bones, turning them from time to time, until golden brown. Pour off the fat into a stock pot. Add the chopped vegetables and sauté until lightly browned. Add the veal bones, parsley, rosemary, sage, and tomatoes. Deglaze the roasting pan with 1 cup (250 mL) of the red wine and then add that to the stock pot. Reduce over medium-high heat to almost nothing, then add another cup (250 mL) of red wine. Repeat. When the wine is reduced to nearly nothing, add 1 quart (1 L) of the veal stock. Reduce by half, then add another quart. Repeat until all the stock has been used. Strain the *jus*, chill, and skim the fat. Keeps 1 week in the fridge or 6 months in the freezer.

Grazie mille Thanks

First I must thank my wife, Roxanne, who once again uncomplainingly endured my obsessive and occasionally ill-tempered state of distraction as I nursed and coaxed another new restaurant—Fabbrica—through its conception, construction, and challenging opening weeks. And then, without pausing for a break or a holiday, immediately started work on a new cookbook all about it.

At the time, a handful of observant critics writing about my new restaurant pointed out that I am not in fact Italian. So there—the cat's out of the bag, and I can no longer, as originally planned, thank Nonna McEwan for showing me my way around an authentic risotto when I was a child of six. To come clean, I picked up the trick of it like most Toronto chefs of my generation, from Franco Prevedello—in my case at Pronto, about thirty years ago. Thanks, Franco, for getting me going with that.

Over the intervening years, there has been a continuous sequence of risottos of one type or another on my menus at North 44, Bymark, and One. There have also been more varieties of hand-rolled pastas and hand-cut ravioli than I or anyone else could possibly count. Innumerable other dishes of Italian origin came and went along with them—and this book draws on that collective experience.

All the same, back in the early planning days for Fabbrica when I sat down with my executive chef, Drew Ellerby, we started mapping out a plan for showcasing Italian cooking of a less conspicuous refinement. For long before I knew the name of this restaurant, I had already decided that its food would be rustic and robustly flavoured. And I wanted pizza to be a part of it.

A few trips to New York later, I decided that my absolute favourite was the seminal, Neapolitan variety, and that its finest example there could be found at Kesté, on Bleecker Street. And since their chef, Roberto Caporuscio, is the American representative of the Associazione Pizzaiuoli Napoletani, and also teaches the craft of authentic Neapolitan pizza making, I sent my chef de cuisine, Rob LeClair, down to work with him for ten long days to get the proper hang of it. Thank you, Roberto, for sharing your secrets—and thank you, Rob, for soaking them up.

As for the rest of the culinary thinking, so many great Italian restaurants from Rome and Venice to London and New York influenced and inspired us that I could not possibly list them all here. But for those of you on a different budget of inquiry who are interested in what my team find best about contemporary Italian cooking, I do recommend four excellent cookbooks, all recently published.

The massive *Made in Italy*, by Giorgio Locatelli, of Locanda Locatelli, in London, England, is a comprehensive masterpiece. *Urban Italian*, the book Andrew Carmellini put together in his New York home kitchen over a year between restaurant gigs, is a great lesson in Italian home cooking and how to achieve culinary brilliance without any counter space. Marco Canora's *Salt to Taste* probably contains more useful insight into culinary method and instinct than you will find in any other cookbook. And finally, Nate Appleman's *A16: Food + Wine* is an impressive testament to what the young chef achieved over his five memorable years at that wonderful restaurant.

First and foremost, I thank Drew and Rob for taking our collective ideas from the planning stage to the restaurant menu, and then assembling the kitchen team to execute it. Of those chefs, I must thank for their especially hard work chef John Kovac and our pastry chef, Sabine Gradauer. Rob, John, and Sabine each had a role in crafting recipes or this book. But for the lion's share of that work I must again thank Drew Ellerby, who took the time day after day to cook these recipes under the careful watch of our collaborator, Jacob

Richler, who then tested them at home and—finally—wrote them down in a manner that any competent home cook can easily comprehend. Thank you, Jacob. For the final piece of the content puzzle, I must thank my sommelier at One, Curtis Elson, for providing all the inspired wine pairing suggestions listed with many recipes.

None of these players could have managed the job without the excellent support of my executive chefs—Brooke McDougall at Bymark, Ivana Raca at McEwan, and Sash Simpson at North 44—and of my management team: thank you, Alyssa Baksh, Cheryl Cartwright, Tiffany Smith Diggins, Jordie McTavish, Tim Salmon, Darlien Scott, and Elaine Viterbo.

As for producing the book itself, I am especially indebted to Andrea Magyar at Penguin Group (Canada), who made it happen. I must also thank her team—especially Penguin's art director, Mary Opper; the production team on the project, including Chrystal Kocher and David Ross; publicity manager Trish Bunnett; and copy-editor Shaun Oakey. Finally, the book would not look nearly as good as it does without the excellent photography of James Tse. Of course, he did not do it alone, so I must also thank food stylist Ruth Gangbar and prop stylist Catherine MacFayden for perfecting the picture.

Thank you, all.

Until next time,
Mark McEwan

Index

About the Author

Mark McEwan is one of Canada's top celebrity chefs. He is also the owner of the highly acclaimed restaurants North 44, Bymark, One, Fabbrica, and the fine food emporium McEwan. McEwan is co-host and head judge on the Food Network's *Top Chef Canada*, host of *The Heat*, and author of *Great Food at Home*. He lives in Toronto.